T0113934

Like-Minds:
Two Hearts, One Mind, One God

Rediscovering the Value of Marriage

JULIEN M. FOLKS

WESTBOW
PRESS®
A DIVISION OF THOMAS NELSON
& ZONDERVAN

WestBow Press books may be ordered through booksellers or by contacting:

WestBow Press
A Division of Thomas Nelson & Zondervan
1663 Liberty Drive
Bloomington, IN 47403
www.westbowpress.com
844-714-3454

ISBN: 978-1-6642-4378-1 (sc)
ISBN: 978-1-6642-4379-8 (hc)
ISBN: 978-1-6642-4377-4 (e)

Library of Congress Control Number: 2021917686

Print information available on the last page.

WestBow Press rev. date: 01/06/2021

~Philippians 2:2 (NKJV) – "fulfill my joy by being like-minded, having the same love, being of one accord of one mind." ~

Contents

Acknowledgments

I first would like to thank my Lord and Savior, Jesus Christ. Without Him, nothing would be possible.

To my entire team at WestBow Press, you guys were vital in bringing together the vision I had with this book. This platform has allowed me to openly share my heart, thoughts, passion, and gift with the world. I cannot thank you guys enough.

I especially what to thank my best friend, partner, and lover of more than eight years, my beautiful wife, Tanisha Folks. Your concept years ago is now the very catalyst of this book. Your support, encouragement, and patience have helped me to cross the finish line of this project. I love you to life, *Sweets*. You are simply the best.

To my friend of nearly 20 years now, Kenneth Brown Jr. Thank you for your encouragement along this journey. You believed in me so much that you found it within your heart to sow a $100.00 seed into supporting this project financially while I was still in the drafting process. That may not be much to some, but the significance of the very act is priceless to me. Thanks, friend.

Lastly, and certainly not least, I want to thank my spiritual family of Word of Life Outreach Ministries of Raleigh, NC, *The Place Where Anything Great Can Happen*. Your prayers and encouragement were never in vain. As a house, I want to thank everyone for helping me in their way in assisting me in magnifying the body of Christ.

Preface

From the moment my wife first mentioned these words: "Like-Minds" while sitting in the living room of our first apartment together as newlyweds back in 2013, the two of us knew we had something valuable. But, boy, did this fresh idea resonate with the two of us. Literally, after only a couple of months into our marriage, while spending much time with God, the two of us discovered a desire to not only share our *coming together* story while encouraging young newlyweds but to exemplify the grace of God operating in the covenant of marriage. Ultimately, *Like-Minds* would be the tool to carry out this mission.

We both perceived, even then, that God had a unique plan for this *fresh idea* that was conceived through the power of agreement in prayer. I can distinctively remember designing our brand's logo and writing down our mission and vision statements during this time. To further promote this *fresh idea*, we thought it was imperative to associate *Like-Minds* with marital seminars hosted by the two of us in our geographical area. Eventually, it would then evolve into its brand. She and I began to price potential venues in our area to accommodate the number of guests we envisioned at these seminars. Then, of course, we took it a step further by thinking of the types of refreshments that would be served, even down to the activities we wanted our couples to participate in at these seminars. Most importantly, together, we brainstormed the vital topics of discussion couples would like to engage in with their spouse. I keenly remember telling Tanisha these words, "We cannot let this die."

Yes, we were passionate and enthusiastic, but were there any *logs for the fire* that would give off the kind of heat that would resonate with a marriage that is on the brink of imploding, leading to a devastating divorce? Were there any tests or challenges we emotionally, mentally, and spiritually endured and overcame together that would provoke hope in another marriage? The answer: "No." Sharing our story of how the two of us got together would not necessarily benefit a marriage suffering from the various *cancers of life*. If anything, it would suffocate it, lacking the receptivity from our focal audience by attempting to stand on a platform both she and I have yet to be conditioned to accept.

I have discovered there is a place right in between our fairytales (e.g., hopes, dreams, and desires) and our nightmares (e.g., loss, pain, and confusion) in which we will all experience at some point; this place is commonly referred to as our reality. Oddly enough, to tell a great story requires a perfect blend of all 3: *fairytale, reality, and nightmares*. The truth of the matter is that there is no better storyteller than Jesus, the expressed image of God. Hebrews 12:2 (NKJV) puts it this way; "Looking unto Jesus the author and finisher of our faith; who for the joy that was set before Him endured the cross, despising the shame, and has sat down at the right hand of the throne of God."

In concert, Romans 8:28 (NKJV), a very familiar passage of scripture, goes on to say, "And we know that all things work together for good to them that love God, to them who are called according to his purpose." In other words, God, Who is eternal, orchestrates from the end to the beginning, giving us grace and a measure of faith to live out our lives according to His Word—this is why Habakkuk 2:4 (NKJV) says, "But the just shall live by his faith."

For perspective, fast-forward to an early Thursday morning of November 2019 while on my drive to work; I heard the voice of God tell me, "Write the book first." I would describe this experience as highly invasive because the desire to get *Like-Minds* off the ground was deeply hidden and buried within my heart. I can recall this event left my heart pounding within my chest as if I had just finished sprinting a 40-yard dash. With tears in my eyes, I remember trying to refocus my attention on the road while traffic streaked by me in the all too familiar morning rush. My only thought: *The God of the Universe just spoke to me.*

I believe God had me revisit what my wife and I held up before Him in prayer over six years before that day. In all honesty, for years, I privately mourned *Like-Minds*, but to my surprise, what appeared to be dead was only sleeping. (Luke 8:52 NKJV) Somewhere along the way, we together had put the mission to sleep by lack of action. Amid all the experiences and challenges she and I overcame in our marriage together, God in His infinite wisdom commanded me on that day to begin planning and writing out the fairytale, reality, and nightmare He had already authored for His glory.

Undoubtedly, we, together in the first seven years of our marriage, have *gathered enough logs* to burn the fire we so desired to create prior. So, I began to type. My wife can attest, without thinking about the finances behind publishing a book or let alone the process; in total faith and obedience, I began to type like an obsessed man.

Early mornings in my old recliner, even before the sun would rise, *I would type.* During my lunch break at work, *I would type.* Late nights on the weekends, *I would type.* Even when I was not writing, I recall ideas, scripture references, and other content that would come to thought so frequently; I would have to pause whatever I was doing to write it down the way it came to me.

By the guidance of the Holy Spirit, He assisted me to write from the place of each *log.* Each *log* symbolizes a trial Tanisha and I faced together while the *fire* represents the grace of God demonstrated throughout each trial. Comparable to the story of the 3 Hebrew boys in the Book of Daniel: *Shadrach, Meshach, and Abednego,* we were not consumed in the midst of what went on between or around us. Spiritually, what resembled an unpromising situation, was actually grace working for us right in our midst. Therefore, we cordially invite you to pull up around the *campfire.*

Dedication

"I dedicate this book to both my natural and spiritual parents: Thaddeus Folks Jr., Eva-Marie Folks of Salisbury, NC, and Dr. Thomas A. DeLoach and Co-Pastor Charise DeLoach of Raleigh, NC. Thank you for your patience, love, discipline, and mentorship throughout the years. Today, I am the man, husband, and father because of you all. Thank you."

Foreword

By Dr. Thomas A. DeLoach

Minister Julien M. Folks is a young, dynamic man of God who loves the Lord, his family, and the church. I've had the profound opportunity of watching him evolve from a young, energetic college student to the man I see today.

For over ten years, Julien patiently worked in learning, improving, and perfecting his craft in the art of serving me in ministry as my righthand man. He has achieved this amid his trials and tribulations, but never without heart and passion for his church, family, and the people he interacts with daily. Every day, he takes the time to become a better husband to his wife and a loving father to his children. His love for his family is unconditional.

As an IT professional, Julien makes sure that every opportunity is a learning experience. He considers his work a blessing that allows him to grow—professionally and personally continuously. Julien likes to stay up to date with the ever-changing world of technology. Whatever is new or uncommon, he finds the time to learn, understand, and apply them. He never stops trying.

In his first book, *Like-Minds: Two Hearts, One Mind, One God—Rediscovering the Value of Marriage,* Julien uses the same strategy that has helped him succeed in his personal life to give you the tools for a great marriage. So many books promise you love and happiness, but they don't give you a practical roadmap to get there. I believe this book does just that.

Marriage can be a wonderful experience, and the author wants you to know that you can have that and more if God is the head of your life—and if you are willing to connect with your spouse at the heart level. Julien takes the time to share his journey and his challenges as a man so that you can be encouraged. He shares his story as a reminder that you can win if you are willing to change no matter where you are.

Another aspect that makes this book stand out is that it is replete with scriptures and Bible stories to anchor his beliefs that God's word is the best solution to a marriage or relationship. I recommend this book to singles wanting to be married, those in pre-marital counseling, and those looking for a refresher on marriage and how you can make the changes necessary to please the Lord.

As you read this book, ask the Holy Spirit to open up your heart so you'll receive a new way to live and become *Two hearts, through One mind, in One God.*

Dr. Thomas A. DeLoach
Founder and Pastor
Word of Life Outreach Ministries – Raleigh, NC

Introduction

I would like to thank you for purchasing my book *Like-Minds: Two hearts, One Mind, One God—Rediscovering the Value of Marriage,* as I believe you, the reader, will capture the attitude of a successful, happy, and lasting marriage. I desire that through these chapters, you will gain clarity on what marriage should be in the kingdom of God and the preparation that is required leading into a full-time commitment with your spouse.

It is not a question that marriages today, especially in this country, are under attack. In my estimation, marriages through the lenses of our nation have significantly lost value and respect amid a growing culture that degraded its significance—this is an epidemic in its own right. *Like-Minds: Two Hearts, One Mind, One God—Rediscovering the Value of Marriage* is a book that attempts to act as a clarion call; to refocus man's attention and heart back to biblical principles carried out by both spouses; rediscovering the value of marriage between that man and woman.

The dynamics of every marriage are different because not one person is the same. Nevertheless, the uniqueness of the individual compliments the marriage, and despite the diversity, *the principles that each marriage honors in return will honor them.*

I have titled this book *Like-Minds: Two Hearts, One Mind, One God—Rediscovering the Value of Marriage* to reference the overall process or journey the man and woman must commit to, permitting them to experience God's overall best in their marriage.

In an attempt to expound a bit, *Two Hearts* symbolizes humanity, the physical and emotional attraction, imperfections, mistakes, and even the willingness of the man and woman to engage with one another. *One Mind* embodies the handling of every presented circumstance by that man and woman together with the mind of Christ. Lastly, *One God* exemplifies both the man and woman's total dependency, reverence, and establishment in God. Each phase is indicative of a lifestyle of its own within any given marriage, which I will further define and bring context later in the book. As the book title suggests, every successful marriage derives from two like-minded individuals whose lives are solidified in the foundation of the Word of God.

To be clear, I am not attempting to give you a *cookie-cutter* approach to a healthy marriage. That is equivalent to telling parents how to raise their young child with strict and overbearing rules and expecting the child to respect them when they get older; chances are very slim, if not nearly impossible. Yet, the excellent advice you receive from family and friends may potentially enhance your instincts to better nurture and raise your child with a better understanding of parenting—shining a light on the significance of the position held.

Ultimately, this is my book's approach—to enhance the ideal perception of this life-long commitment in hopes to show the undeniable value of sustaining God's institution of marriage. You will discover that what is often enhanced is valued.

Because you now have this book, I assume you are either a single, curious as to what marriage should be like, a young couple planning on getting married, or a married couple simply desiring to gain a better understanding of marriage. Whatever background you may see yourself coming from, let us build from there together. The personal experiences and principles of the Word of God that will be shared in this book are intended to bring a *renewed appreciation and value* of God's divine creation—the union between God's man and woman. As with everything else in life, if you see something as valuable, you will treat it as such. *It is my deepest prayer and greatest desire that each reader will take away from my transparency and candidness and observe the grace of God operating within a marriage when both husband and wife are like-minded in Christ.*

What is Marriage?

*"People are weird. When we find someone
with weirdness that is compatible with
ours, we team up and call it love."*

~ Dr. Seuss

At a very young age, at least in the Western culture, it is almost natural for little girls to dream of their prince charming to one day sweep them off their feet and to live together in their dream-like palace living happily ever after. For every beautiful fairytale princess, an attractive and charming young prince will come along to *save the day*. As in many fairytales, the two will first meet in some downtown marketplace; they lock eyes, and there is almost an instantaneous and infectious strong connection at first sight. You guessed it: they are in love—no doubt about it. Birds sing a melody, *the blue skies are bluer, and the green grass is greener.* Yes, *in living color* at its finest. The two can already hear the wedding bells ringing louder than their thoughts and heartbeat. There is a song that only the two of them know in which they sing harmoniously together. Right on cue, prince charming finally builds up enough courage to ask the princess' hand in marriage. As she eagerly says "yes," the orchestra comes in gently, playing the all too familiar *Love Theme from Romeo and Juliet Overture.* Days later, there is a huge wedding, and it appears the whole town is in attendance. The two ride off happily ever after in their *horse and carriage,* with hundreds applauding and congratulating them. The credits begin to roll.

Barbie and Ken

I understand that I may have been a bit over the top, but hopefully, you could connect with the visual. When dating someone new, it is natural to feel overly excited and anxious to get to know the opposite sex personally. In most cases, the man and woman are in a euphoric place emotionally when dating. In these moments, the brain is constantly inundated with endorphins—this is what I like to describe as the *Barbie and Ken* mirage. The woman only *sees her Ken,* while the man only *sees his Barbie.* The two are both stimulated by *accessories* and other *compliments* alike. But, then, almost as quick as blood rushes to one's face while blushing, the *wedding* for the two has been scheduled and planned, while the *marriage,* unfortunately, was never truly considered.

Here is the biggest misconception; many have mistakenly considered their wedding as their *marriage.* Often, the wedding, which is the ceremonial event, appears to be so captivating, many run to this event like a mass exodus in hopes to partake of *the land flowing with milk and honey* on the other side. In all fairness, it is to be expected. It is the wedding that has bride and groom as the focal point, but if we are sincere, it is without a doubt the bride's day—sorry, fellas. Please, do not forget about the bride in her dress. Do you recall the time and money invested in picking out the right one? The bride in her dress demands attention; the bride in her dress will get the attention.

Family and friends are there to witness the coming together of man and woman on this joyous occasion. First, there is an exchange of rings and wedding vows. Followed up with the question by the marriage officiant, in which the two answer with, "I do." Then, there are smiles, applauds, and special remarks from family and friends during the reception. Yes, that's right, there is no wedding celebration without a reception. Once the DJ spins the music, everyone, including Granny and Granddad, is all out on the dance floor, busting their best dance moves.

Now, by no means am I making a mockery of weddings. On the contrary, I think weddings are beautiful events that should remind everyone in attendance why that remarkable man and woman are coming together. However, to proceed forward, it is essential to see marriage as a life-long commitment and not as a single life event one circles on their calendar. Distinguishing the difference between a marriage and a wedding helps keep the bond the two have for one another in its proper perspective.

So What Is It?

So, what exactly is marriage? I would define marriage as a holy and sacred union between man and woman, ordained by God. Throughout scripture, we will learn that anything holy and sacred is set apart for God's use. So, yes, God has created and ordained marriage between a man and woman specifically for His use. Let that settle in. It is this kind of thinking that provokes an awareness of accountability from both husband and wife. But to know God's use for marriage, one must understand the perfect will of God.

To begin, Genesis 2:24 (NKJV) states, "Therefore a man shall leave his father and his mother and hold fast to his wife, and they shall become one flesh." I think this carries great significance because the author clearly states, "shall become," which denotes a future expression. Did you get that? This passage of scripture validates and echoes the idea that *your wedding day* is not *your marriage.* The marriage between man and woman is a constant life-long meshing of flesh—two different ways of thinking .. two egos .. two attitudes .. two people. So yes, if you are a young married couple, disagreements are simply an indication of the process in operation. Just stand in there.

Of course, the flesh is constantly fighting for what it has deemed as valuable: *itself.* To bring context, in Ephesians 5:22—25 (NKJV), we see that the wife must submit, whereas the husband must give up himself. To put it plainly, he must die. Ouch! Marriage is a perfect waltz of flesh constantly submitting and dying. This process requires work and commitment. I mean, who in their right mind would want to commit to a life-long commitment of *submitting and dying?* Answer: Only those who want to work. As my spiritual father and pastor, Dr. Thomas A. DeLoach, once put it, "If you do not like to work, do not get married." A marriage will not sustain unless two people put forth the work.

It is important to note that marriage is only as strong as the Word of God the two choose to build on. It is God's Word, His thoughts that reveal and remind God's promises to both husband and wife even when the love between the two seems to be evaporating from the two in heated moments. Yes, I am talking about *iron hot* heated moments; the *stove is on HIGH* heated moments.

But in all seriousness, if the husband knows he should love his wife, just as Christ loved the church, according to Ephesians 5:25 (NKJV)—the husband would then exemplify his belief into action. Not only would this create an atmosphere of unity in the home but a solid foundation to stand on. Likewise, if the wife knows she should respect her husband according to Ephesians 5:33 (NKJV), she would exemplify her belief into action. Eventually, this act of obedience provokes trust in his leadership and covering as a husband. The

Word of God is a book full of principles that do not restrict our *freedom* in marriage by any stretch of the imagination; instead, it is there to protect it.

As of this writing, according to the American Psychological Association, nearly 40 to 50 percent of married couples in the United States are now divorced. (Why Divorce Is So Common in Today's Society (The Sad Truth), Justin Tash. 2021.)

What is more alarming, according to other studies from a professor and sociologist of the University of Connecticut, Bradley Wright, for people who identify themselves as Christians or of the faith, 60% of married couples have ended in divorce. (Divorce Rate in the Church – As High as the World, Glenn T.Stanto. 2011.)

What is going on here? This fact should be a red flag of great concern for any married couple and single person. As briefly stated in the preface of this book, there are, for the most part, three classifications of a marriage that is most prominent in today's culture (as there are many categories that would not be within the scope of this book):

1. A *successful* marriage: can be defined as one that has lasted despite the obstacles due to the preparation and rehearsal of marital tools given by an honorable life coach, pastor, or professional marital counselor.

2. A *failed* marriage: can be defined as one that could not overcome obstacles due to either negligence of the preparation that requires a new life of commitment to a new spouse; abandoning to rehearse the tools from pre-marital counseling, or lastly from ignorance; never walking into the understanding of marriage.

3. A *stagnant* marriage, more commonly known as a *broken* marriage: can be defined as one that has lasted; however, the two have found contentment in dysfunction or unproductiveness in the marriage.

Two Like-Minded Individuals

No marriage has all the answers, which is why professionals such as a life coach, pastor, or marital counselor can efficiently assist in vital areas such as communication between spouses, patterns of emotional behaviors, forgiveness, or even finances in the embryonic stages of the marriage.

Which opens the floor for one question: How is *success* defined in the interest of a marriage? Well, one will have to define their *success* and see if their definition aligns with the Word of God honestly and wholeheartedly. In Joshua 1:8 (NKJV), it reads, "This Book of the Law shall not depart from your mouth, but you shall meditate in it day and night, that you may observe to do according to all that is written in it. For then you will make your way prosperous, and then you will have good success." According to the scripture, *success* is contingent on the individual's lifestyle. For instance, if I needed to know an individual's lifestyle, I would first listen to their daily conversation. This skill gives insight into what they think about day and night. This charts out how prosperous an individual is in whatever they do. Marriage is essentially a new lifestyle of thinking about what is best for the two.

One might ask, should a successful marriage be defined by the luxuries of life, like a new house or car? Maybe there is a marriage whose success is sending their four teens off to college debt-free? Or perhaps, another marriage's success could be traveling to any part of the world at leisure? Who in their right mind would not want to experience these significant life milestones? Now, would you say these marriages are successful? Absolutely and without question. According to these marriages, if you were to ask each couple if they were successful, chances are they would all agree they have undoubtedly met their goals.

Yes, goal setting is an excellent way to measure success. I agree with this idea. Unfortunately, nearly all manufactured items or achievements can and will depreciate over the years. Children grow older and start families of their own; traveling now becomes mundane as you get older. The marriage that was once defined by the numerous goals in life is now represented by former glory. Tragically, the husband and wife are now in pursuit in searching to fill a void that is not obtained externally; instead, only in a foundation the two never considered building on from the start. If we were to consider every *benchmark of success,* you would note none were spiritual investments into the actual marriage. In other words, what feeds a marriage, which is a spirit of itself, is *spiritual nourishment.* If there is no spiritual sustenance that constantly finds its way back into a marriage, like a plant without proper nutrients, it will soon wither and die.

This thought leads me to our next marriage classification, a failed marriage that did not last when faced with challenging obstacles. Again, these types of marriages end by either: *negligence of the preparation that requires for a new life of commitment to their new spouse, by abandoning to rehearse the tools from pre-marital counseling, or lastly from ignorance, which is never stepping into the understanding of what marriage is or its purpose.* Most, if not all, marriages fail due to some variation of one of these three arguments. When observing a failed marriage, one would notice that every *cause of failure* implies that either the husband or wife has ceased making the necessary investments and adjustments to the overall health of that marriage.

In no way do I or my wife believe that any husband or wife, who at one time in love with each other suddenly *fall out of love or grow apart.* The London Bridge does not suddenly fall all at once. Usually, in this all too familiar instance, there were erroneous decisions made by a spouse that preceded the emotional disconnect the two are now experiencing. These decisions often derive from vindictive, unforgiving, or wayward thinking—the recipe for divorce. When the heart of either spouse sets to revenge or unforgiveness, it is nearly impossible to remain and live *with* the daily reminder of discontent.

Disastrously, the separation appears to be the best resolution to the matter.

This idea leaves us to our last classification of a marriage often portrayed in our culture—a stagnant marriage that lasted; nonetheless, the two are now painfully unhappy. Again, this marriage is synonymous with a *broken marriage,* a term that is all too familiar. Unfortunately, the two have found contentment amid dysfunction or unproductiveness. It is very similar to the unsuccessful/failed marriage; here, the two are now just co-existing and questioning whether it will work or, even worse, whether the two are right for one another. Despite popular belief, it is vital to note that stagnant or *broken marriages* can still be salvaged and repaired, hence *broken* marriage. With the proper conversation in a safe place, such as in counseling, my wife and I believe that issues can be resolved—contingent on full participation from both spouses.

Commonly, it is these stagnant-broken marriages that are cultivated by either pressure or by way of convenience. That is, a compulsive decision to get married seems to be the most convenient way to bring some resolve to a financial or personal matter. Or perhaps by the strong influences from family and friends, which may have been the sole reason that man and woman decided to join initially. I suspect pressure has got to be "Public Enemy #1" against most marriages. I believe it is the very catalyst that dictates a lot of unprepared couples into lifetime commitments unknowingly.

If you have lived for any amount of time, I'm sure you may have heard of at least one of these before: "You haven't found anyone yet?", "When will I get my first grandchild?", "When will you finally settle down?", "You are not getting any younger." I have found that these questions and statements push couples into lifetime prisons with total strangers; rather than in lifetime successful marriages with life partners. The two involved must then live up to the erratic standards, opinions, and suggestions of others. Consequently, when the marriage crumbles, the two are only left with the unfilled expectations of others, with the fear of embarrassment from their close circle.

At this point, the image the two desperately try to protect and hold onto in the face of family, friends, peers, or even within the church community appears to be their priority. Perhaps children are involved, and staying together seems most favorable for the children's sake. But, no matter how determined the two attempt to *save face* within their circle, one thing is for certain—it will require full participation to remove every hindrance and *create new rivers of life* back into that same marriage.

What is the Purpose of Marriage?

As stated earlier in this chapter, God has ordained marriage between a man and woman for a divine purpose. Well, what exactly is the purpose of marriage? This question is not necessarily a popular question to ask, nor is it a popular question to answer. Often, the purpose of marriage is *swept under the rug* due to its stigma in the general public. The reasoning: "There can't possibly be purpose in what is considered a gamble or risk, can it?" Having a firm and clear perspective of what a marriage is intended for leaves room for any young couple to consider their preparation for the next chapter of their lives.

Indeed, with all the intricate and delicate aspects of marriage, there must have been something God had in mind when joining man and woman together, right? The obvious approach is to start at the beginning, in Genesis. The Bible declares in Genesis 1:27—28 (NKJV) that "So God created man in His own image; in the image of God He created Him; male and female He created them." Here we see that man and woman is a spirit. They were created out of a Spirit—Who is God the Father. The following verse states, "Then

God blessed them, and God said to them, "Be fruitful and multiply; fill the earth and subdue it."

At first thought, you would assume God only refers to having children through procreation to fill the earth. Not so. (I will discuss the significance of procreation in Chapter 6-Sex: Its Origin and Identity) God also refers to replicating His Spirit, His spiritual DNA, His fingerprint throughout the earth with man and woman. However, the only way to do both is to create a physical vessel by which fulfilling this request could be carried out accordingly. So, in Genesis 2:7 (NKJV), we see God is now forming *man; as in Adam*, from the dust, then breathed into his nostrils; man became a living being.

In Genesis 2:18 (NKJV), we see God has created His creation, man; however, the only dilemma is man is alone. According to scripture, God says, "It is not good that man should be alone; I will make him a helper comparable to him." Someone equal in quality and which no other creature in his environment can complement his likeness. Here is where things get interesting. In Genesis 2:21(NKJV), the Bible states God caused a *deep-deep* sleep on Adam. He then reached inside Adam, took out one of his ribs, and closed the flesh in its place—this is very important because God never found it necessary to go back inside Adam again to take another rib once he closed him up. Think about that. God went inside Adam once and retrieved what Adam needed: *his help*, indicative of when God is in the process of joining man and woman together; it is intended to be final and with great purpose.

We then see the hands of God fashioning Adam's rib into woman, *a man with a womb, a masterpiece, a delight to behold, with curves, an instant attraction.* "Come on, men. Follow me." Good news, fellas, he now has someone to join to and call wife, according to Genesis 2:24 (NKJV). Here is the first time we see the term *wife* in the scripture. The meshing of two has now begun. However, recall that the instructions God gave *man and woman* still reverberates from out of the *spirit of this union.* God still expects man and woman to "be fruitful and multiply; fill the earth and subdue it."

Everything that God creates has a purpose to fulfill. You strip away a creation's purpose, and it is no longer happy. I can go further on to say the creation is a *failure*. Like a bird's purpose is to fly the vast skies or a fish's purpose is to swim the deep seas, a marriage's divine purpose is to *multiply God's image and likeness here on earth, where two are working together in unison*. Adam's wife, his *help;* coming alongside him together in marriage to leave the very fingerprint of God in the same earth from which he was fashioned.

Think about that, a lasting impression for others to see that God was glorified right here on the *earth* through a holy union; with God's man and woman. I believe this to be so encouraging and powerful because it says God only creates with great intentions. This, my friend, should give you, and I hope. This is why divorce can potentially distort the *image* of God here on earth and abort the ultimate mission, which is to "be fruitful and multiply; fill the earth and subdue it."

Multiplying God's Image
and Likeness

What does this even look like or entail? What does a marriage *multiplying God's image and likeness* here on earth even mean? First, both husband and wife need to have a constant prayer life—this is vital. There is nothing more intimate than husband and wife coming together in prayer. I believe as one is praying, the other one should be listening and touching in agreement. My wife and I believe the idea of *Like-Minds* was conceived out of simply being open in prayer as to what God had in store for us. Within the first year of our marriage, we knew this *Like-Minds* idea would be used as a catalyst to glorify God somehow out of the union He alone orchestrated. But, at that time, we did not know how entirely. This book you are now reading is associated with our assignment, infectiously spreading God's image and likeness here on earth; by way of giving a young married couple hope that has lost hope and providing a single person a marital perspective while preparing for that next chapter of a lifetime commitment.

So, to clarify, when a marriage multiplies God's image and likeness here on earth, it is taking what God has revealed to that marriage and maximizing that vision's potential. For some marriages, it could be starting up a neighborhood food pantry, planting a local church, publishing a book, organizing marital seminars, a homeless shelter, after-school programs, non-profit organizations, etc. These examples echo empowerment within a union orchestrated by the will of God for the entire world to witness. The sight alone, man and woman, husband, and wife, standing together as a unit says to the world God cares, and God does love His people. Through these avenues, people not only hear the compassion of God, but they are then able to partake in His *compassion* as well.

Now one may be thinking to themselves, "Are you saying a single person filled with the Holy Spirit cannot create a lasting impact on the earth?" Why, of course not, they most certainly can. The Bible is full of numerous stories in which God used either a single man or woman to play a significant role in spreading the Gospel whereby they operated. If God can use a donkey, he most certainly can use a single person. However, when looking at the creation, you must also consider its overall purpose. When God looked at a single Adam in the Garden of Eden, his only purpose was to *tend* and *keep it*. Let's begin to look into this further.

Tending and Keeping

God provided the rain for the garden, but there was no man to till it. An opportunity has now presented itself. God then places this single man amid his purpose. Adam finds contentment in this *place*. But I think there is something else worth paying close attention to here. The words *tend* and *keep* allude that one must *guard* and *protect* what is valuable. It is no surprise that God would find it fitting for a *single person* to have this task. Okay, so I think by now you know where I am going with this.

Yes, I can address here that practicing abstinence is part of this *tending* and *keeping* responsibility God has given each single—this should provide singles everywhere with hope. In this frame of mind, a single person is spiritually developing and maturing while focusing solely on their relationship with God, their Father.

This truth undoubtedly initiates a lasting impact on the earth because, unfortunately, practicing abstinence before marriage is extremely rare; in some cases, mocked or even frowned upon in our culture. Thus, one would be considered *abnormal* or *unusual* by today's standards. Nevertheless, understanding this philosophy makes the process not only possible but easier when either that man or woman knows their *sense of worth, identity, and work*.

The question that every single must answer for themselves is, "Am I content on maintaining what has been given to me?" This self-reflective question takes precedence over just *wanting to get married*. For the record, single Adam never wanted to join anyone in marriage; actually, it was his contentment that attracted God's attention. Think about that for a moment. Much like the garden, God created and entrusted a body to us to *keep* and *tend* until marriage. 1 Corinthians 6:19 (NKJV) tells us, "Or do you not know that your bodies are temples of the Holy Spirit, who is in you, whom you have received from God, and you are not your own?" This process should not be a daunting task; instead, it should highlight the accountability placed on that single individual.

However, here is where things shift a bit for single Adam. When God looked at Adam again in Genesis 2:18 (NKJV), He says, not to Adam, but Himself, "It is not good for man to be alone; I will make him a helper comparable to him." As stated earlier, Adam has God's attention. Touchdown with the extra point! Since God is omniscient, meaning as the Creator and Narrator of life, He knows everything; He considered the overall purpose of marriage; His creation. To be fruitful, multiply, and subdue implies that there first must be an established union between a man and woman. Thus, anytime God referenced words like "fruitful," "multiply," and even "subdue" in Eden, He would always allude to man and woman working together.

It Takes Two Baby!

So yes, in the words of one of hip-hop's greatest duos—Rob Base and DJ EZ Rock, "It Takes Two." There is no doubt about it. Ecclesiastes 4:9—10 (NKJV) reads, "Two are better than one because they have a good return for their labor. For if they fall, one will lift up his companion. But woe to him who is alone when he falls, for he has no one to help him up." So, due to the task ordained by God for marriage, God constructed within His creation a compensation plan.

In a partnership, if one of the partners becomes weak, weary, sick, falls away, discouraged, or frustrated with God's plan, "one can help the other up" (Ecclesiastes 4:9—10 NKJV). As I stated before, this is contingent on the foundation of faith that the two have built. In this gift of helping the other up, one reminds the other that the two together have a "good return for their labor."

We have now defined marriage, its origin, and purpose, giving us a healthy and holistic outlook of God's ordained creation. Because marriage is a created entity by God, it has a spirit—it has a life. Every life needs to be fed and nurtured, but most importantly, it needs God, the Sustainer, and Giver of that life.

God is essentially the foundation of marriage and its existence, the center from which it operates, and there is no marriage without God. Excluding God from marriage is like a withdrawn child who moves out from under their guardian's roof prematurely and is no longer under their protection and care. The child perceived this protection as a restriction. In turn, it provoked them to leave from under the guardian's *covering* in an attempt to try things *their* way.

This analogy illustrates the separation of life from the Life-Giver and expecting to thrive and live. How long do you expect that *child* to make it without yearning for their previous environment? Not long. Even nature proves this theory; plants do not do so well without the proper nourishment from the soil. They will soon wither and die. In the protection and care of the *parent*, we find the much-needed correction, instructions, and even the encouragement to enable the child to develop, stand, and walk on into maturity. Again, marriage is a life, which is why we often hear the term "marriage-life." How well you benefit from your marriage is contingent on how well you care for your marriage.

We must then look at marriage as a life to develop for and a life that requires a whole new way of thinking. Remember, Adam was equipped for marriage because he was content *tending* and *keeping* the garden God left to him. Certain qualities, such as commitment, were instilled in him as he focused on *his work*. Adam acquired a quality of commitment amid his contentment. Did you get that? Friend, this can only be found right in the place where God dropped him, *in phase one* right there in the garden.

To rush into a *marriage life* without the preparation, tools, or regard for what God has deemed holy; results in the likelihood of two of the discussed categories of marriages. Much like the child that has willfully withdrawn from their parents, there is no space to mature in the way the parents best see fit—the relationship is considered broken.

Making Decisions from a Broken Relationship with God

What is considered broken ceases to identify anything of great worth. Take, for instance, a vending machine with a sign that says OUT OF ORDER. Though it is designed to receive $1.00 bills, it is for the moment incapable of *recognizing* its value. In other words, to identify the $1.00 bill, there needs to be repairs or adjustments to correct the error. As it relates to a man and woman rushing into a lifetime commitment, many irrational decisions are made from this place of brokenness; both are incapable of seeing the value in one another, let alone the overall marriage. The immaturity or the rebelliousness of that man or woman often influences the two to walk down a path that seems right, but its end is the way to death. (Proverbs 14:12—NKJV) Their reasoning or better judgment is ignored, and the couple erroneously refers to marriage.

Rather than falling in love with *God's intent of that marriage*, it would appear that falling in love with the *idea of marriage* seems to be more satisfactory. Neglecting God's way of building a strong, healthy, and lasting marriage and expecting the blessings and benefits of God's creation is impossible.

Let me put it like this: the wife in the state of rebellion should *not expect* her rebellious husband to love her as Christ loved the church and gave Himself up for her, as Ephesians 5:25 (NKJV) states. To add insult to injury, the husband in this same state is incapable of knowing God's precepts if he is no longer in a place where he can hear from God.

In short, the love of God is perfect and wholesome. 1 Corinthians 13:4—8 (NKJV) tells us, "Love suffers long and is kind; love does not envy; love does not parade itself, is not puffed up; does not behave rudely, does not seek its own, is not provoked, thinks no evil; does not rejoice in iniquity, but rejoices in the truth; bears all things, believes all things, hopes all things, endures all things. Love never fails. But whatever there are prophecies, they will fail; whether there are tongues, they will cease; whether there is knowledge, it will vanish away." Without acknowledging and accepting this biblical truth from both spouses, the risk of making permanent decisions based on temporary emotions is more likely to occur.

As we come to the end of this chapter, questions come to mind: What do you call a union between man and woman without the

Spirit of God? What are expectations from both man and woman if God is not the primary factor in joining together? How long do the two believe the union will survive without God in the picture? These are the type of questions one must ask before diving headfirst into a lifetime commitment and expecting God's provision in return. Provision from God is only as perfect as the obedience of the individual. That is what marriage is; adherence within the confines of God perfect, matchless, and sovereign will. Husband and wife are learning to live together in unison under the umbrella of God's perfect love, protection, and provision.

"Like-Mind Connection" Wrap-Up:

1. How would you classify your marriage? Could it be anything other than a successful marriage? If so, how are you and your spouse planning to improve?
2. In what ways are you and your spouse multiplying God's image and likeness?
3. For the single, what would be your expectations coming into your marriage? For the married couple, what are the expectations of your marriage now?

Husband as Priest in Home

"We Must Protect This House"

~ UNDER ARMOUR

In 2006, you may recall a commercial by Under Armour, a company internationally known for its sports apparel. It spawned athletes from everywhere to be motivated by their most appealing slogan yet: *We Must Protect This House*. Of course, this slogan single handily fueled the competitive nature every true athlete commonly shares before facing their opponent. But, more importantly, the message addresses the idea: "Never allow your opponent to defeat you in your own house."

To attempt to bring context here, in the commercial, viewers will observe former NFL player Eric Ogbogu, aka "Big E," rallying other teammates while they are mentally and physically preparing for the battle ahead inside their home training facility. As a visual, the commercial descriptively expresses the determination that the entire team has all fed into: *We Must Protect This House*. In the commercial, viewers will see the familiar hand clapping of teammates, weight spotting, the taunting of trainers, gym fans blowing, the grunting of men lifting and dropping heavyweights on the gym floor, sweat dripping from the face and body of nearly every athlete. One would say this is the ideal atmosphere of dedication and discipline that produces champions and winners alike. Certainly, what is depicted in these scenes is not mere emotion but a belief system that every teammate has prepared to display on game day. I mean, who would not want to go to battle with this kind of belief?

The Priestly Anointing

As men who take on many roles and responsibilities, *Protecting Your House* as a priest is a mandate and priority when walking with God inside the household. To effectively carry out the various roles, there needs to be an anointing that a High Priest can only give. Ephesians 5:22—24 (NKJV) says, "Wives, submit yourselves to your own husbands as you do to the Lord. For the husband is the head of the wife as Christ is the head of the church, his body, of which he is the Savior of the body. Therefore, just as the church is subject to Christ, so let the wives be to their own husbands in everything." In biblical times, it was a custom in the Hebrew practice for the high priests to anoint an individual's head with oil and to allow it to run downward. This act was an outward demonstration to the public that said not only is God's hand on that person, but they have been divinely selected to accomplish a task for God.

In God's marriage covenant, the anointing comes into contact with the *head* first, then the body. In other words, whatever the head receives, the body will also receive in significant proportions. To be clear, this does not discredit the anointing that the woman had before coming into a marriage—it adds value to the marriage; however, what should be essential to bear in mind is when she becomes married, her husband now becomes her *head*. As I mentioned in the previous chapter, this biblical principle is often controversial in Christendom because marriage is a perfect waltz of submitting and dying. Therefore, anything that has *two heads* is not only a monster, but that entity has now become profane. Therefore, as a husband, as head, your positioning or relationship with God is paramount. Though this scripture denotes husbands as priests of their home, this responsibility is not automatic as it may appear to be. Recall the Under Armour commercial; the men fed into the belief that their home, their position was worth protecting. They were keenly aware of what was at stake should they taste defeat in their own home. So, what did they do? They trained … and trained … and trained. Again, *We Must Protect This House* is a mandate — a demand carried out by spiritual discernment, not by impulse.

Adding Value to the Marriage

Personally, within the first year of our marriage, this concept was difficult for me to grasp and carry out because I did not know what was at stake. At the time, I admit I could not carry out the idea of the principle from my head into action. As a husband, priest; learning your responsibility does take time and great patience. In the beginning, I became prone to make irrational decisions in pressured moments that could have altered the trajectory of our marriage, home, and lifestyle. It was some of the significant wrinkles I had to iron out over time by the grace of God. I recall an instance in which I reluctantly worked 12-hour night shifts for an international IT company. Due to the toll it had on my body and the demand it required of me, I impulsively emailed my wife from work that I was putting in my resignation papers to find employment elsewhere as a fork lifter. Yup. Easy escape. Now, in no way am I attempting to belittle this profession; nevertheless, I knew this was not the plan God had for me; I wanted out. Anywhere but that job. I was at my wit's end.

So, I did what any immature, *spiritual* newlywed husband would do; conjure up some false-religious lie and hope that my newlywed wife would accept it like bait. Thinking, "Yes, that would work. She will completely understand, right?" Well, it backfired. It is a good thing I married someone with spiritual discernment; (recall I mentioned the anointing of the wife adds value to the marriage), the anointing that could identify the error of misjudgment and even my rebellious behavior. Tanisha said something to me that resonated with me until this day. She said, "I am sorry, I cannot follow that." Ouch, right in the gut. I gained an even greater respect for her when she addressed me in the manner she did so that I would grasp if you know what I mean. The conversation that followed was not only needed, but it was also indicative of the fact my *head* was not appropriately aligned to receive the anointing from our High Priest for our marriage. I needed adjustment.

Priestly Roles

For every husband reading this now, your effectiveness can only go as far as your humility. Humility affects every aspect of your life, including your marriage. When researching the word *humility*, I found that it derives from the Latin word *humilitas*, a noun closely related to the adjective *humilis*. Hence, here is where we get the word *humus*, which means *grounded* or *from the earth*. Unless the husband *lowers* himself and submits himself to God, he cannot come under any anointing. To put it plainly, the husband becomes inadequate in carrying out his role as priest and husband in his home. *I Must Protect This House* remains only a fabricated idea to him, never his obligation.

From a biblical perspective, it would be necessary to address the priestly roles given to someone in this position. As one would imagine, the priest's role is to reflect on God and act as the intercessor or mediator between God and His people. Traditionally, the priest would not go into God's presence empty-handed; instead, they would often take with them an offering on behalf of God's people; usually, a calf or dove signifying the trespasses and sins of the people. While doing so, the priests would begin to present God with prayer, praise, and thankfulness. This act would attract the Spirit of God to meet the people right where they were.

Ultimately, God wants to abide wherever His Spirit is. So a priest, the husband, should act as this mediator between God and his home. This invitation or *wooing* of God is initiated by the husband presenting God daily with prayer, praise, and thankfulness as the priests did while going up before the altar of God. Not only does this creates the atmosphere in that man's home, but it also produces a steady climate for him and his family to function accordingly.

In Numbers 18:5 (NKJV), we see the Lord specifically assigns His priests roles for him to fulfill. The Lord tells Aaron, his high priest, "And you shall attend to the duties of the sanctuary and the duties of the altar, that there may be no more wrath on the children of Israel." Do you hear the weight of that statement? Essentially, Aaron is responsible for taking *care* of the sanctuary and the altar by ensuring God's Spirit abides in that place. Meaning, Aaron has the great responsibility *to be on guard* and *watch* what is sacred, take care of the place where God will constantly speak, and his servant can always listen. Virtually, this is the posture in which every man of God should take in *his sanctuary*.

The Strong Man

What comes to mind when you hear *strong man?* If you are anything like me, you may picture an Arnold Schwarzeneggar or a Vin Diesel type of character who displays characteristics of heroism on levels one can only imagine. Like in the action movies, I am willing to bet, fighting one on one with either of these two, you would have a slim chance of coming out as the victor. I have watched too many *Terminator* and *The Fast and the Furious* fighting scenes to know this to be true. Somehow these heroes manage to find themselves escaping some of the most unpromising situations. On the other hand, if either the *Terminator* or *Dominic* type of character is outnumbered 1 to 10, the movie's ending may have a completely different outcome. That hero, that strong man, would more than likely be counted as a casualty.

The Bible clearly describes this action scene for us in a couple of places in scripture: Mark 3:27 (NKJV) and Luke 11:24—28 (NKJV). Mark 3:27 (NKJV) says, "No one can enter a strong man's house and plunder his goods unless he first binds the strong man. And then he will plunder his house." One of the underlining factors that are so common in the body of Christ is men unwilling to take on priestly duties in their homes due to personal bondage. Bondage of addictions such as *substance abuse, pornography, anger, work, or even pride.* How can you expect a man or anyone, for that matter, to do the things of God bound?

Fighting the Invisible

This first action scene, Mark 3:27 (NKJV), alludes to the idea of another *man* binding up our hero, The Terminator, and spoiling his dwelling place. Now, you may be wondering, "What on earth can bind up The Terminator?" Simple. An entity in which he cannot see: *an evil spirit.* This *man* in which Mark 3:27 (NKJV) is referring to is not the same *man* we see in Genesis 1:27 (NKJV) that states, "So God created man in His own image, in the image of God created he him; male and female created He them." For clarity, in Genesis, *man* in Greek is "Anthropos," which applies to both genders, male and female, while in Mark 3:27 (NKJV), *man* is perceived as an *unclean* spirit. An unclean spirit is any spirit that is contrary to the Spirit of God. But what makes this *man* or unclean spirit powerful enough to subdue our hero? Great question. I will address it momentarily.

But first, if we *grab our remotes and tune into* Luke 11:24—28 (NKJV), we will now see our second hero, Dominic, in a very similar action scene as the Terminator. This passage says, "When an unclean spirit goes out of a man, he goes through dry places, seeking rest; and finding none, he says, "I will return to my house from which I came." And when he comes, he finds it swept and put in order. Then he goes and takes with him seven other spirits more wicked than himself, and they enter and dwell there, and the last state of that man is worse than the first." Here, we should identify that our hero, at one point, recently recovered from a recent fight scene. However, our hero was bound by an *influence,* and let's say; he was not on his "A" game.

We all can somehow relate to this at a point in our lives. However, scripture says that after our strong man's recovery, he is delivered by the God of our salvation, El Yeshuati (from yeshuah meaning victory, deliverance). This "unclean spirit goes out of the man, he goes through dry places, seeking rest; and finding none, he says, "I will return to my house from which I came." This passage of scripture suggests unclean spirits do reason within themselves and are very territorial over your possessions.

Place of Victory

Notice that the *unclean spirit* finds the strong man's soul *swept and put in order,* but there is no strong man, no priest that it sees; only a strong man's unfinished work. There is no one occupying or residing in that place of victory. Let that sink in for a moment. We see that this indicates that there was progress, but the strong man, for whatever reason, has forfeited his *place of victory.* As a priest, and the strong man of our homes, the work we abandon is an unclean spirit's opportunity to destroy. Simply put, abandonment is the enemy's platform to destroy our most precious goods: *our marriages, children, relationships, ministry, finances, and even our health.*

Adverting our attention back to our question: "What makes this *man* or *unclean spirit* powerful enough to subdue our hero?" Answer: "seven other spirits more wicked than himself." Our Terminator is outnumbered by enemies he cannot see—this is a double whammy. He is taking blows from every angle without any clues as to where they are coming from; this is a fighting scene no man wants to find himself in. Unfortunately, this is the fight scene many great men privately wrestle with daily. The mismanagement of our *souls* triggers the enemy to take up residence in our *souls and our homes. We Must Protect This House* now takes on a whole new meaning. It should provoke you and me as priests of our homes to leave the place of damage control and live and remain in a position of being proactive in the things of God.

Matter of the Heart

It is essentially impossible to force a person to do anything they are just not willing to do. As husbands and priests, we must discipline ourselves to perform the duties and responsibilities in our homes — it is a prerequisite. So often, the word *discipline* for men reminds us of work in the natural rather than a spiritual privilege. Tragically, far too often, men tend to run away from discipline due to the stigma it brings with it. Discipline denotes *regulations* and *order*, two elements every man needs in his life but would instead put off to later in life. The church represents this *discipline*, which is why a great percentage of men appear to be missing in Sunday gatherings across this country.

To attempt to go a little deeper. The word *disciple,* meaning *a follower* or *student,* derives from the word discipline. To put it plainly, to be disciplined means to have self-control with great consistency and persistence. For context, following God requires individuals to exemplify a level of discipline somewhere in their daily walk of life. If we look at Mark 1:16—18 (NKJV), we will see this very idea demonstrated. Scripture says, "And as He walked by the Sea of Galilee, He saw Simon and Andrew his brother casting a net into the sea; for they were fishermen. Then Jesus said to them, "Follow Me, and I will make you become fishers of men." They immediately left their nets and followed Him." It may be well-argued that what single-handedly *caught* Simon and Andrew out of a sea of men was their level of discipline. Other fishermen in the surrounding area may have been doing similar work as these men, but can we say their *discipline* measured up?

Level of Discipline

This idea epitomizes men in Christendom as it relates to discipline in every facet of our lives. If we were to consider the level of discipline we exemplify, where exactly would you and I measure up? Discipline is solely a matter of the heart. We will see in Matthew 15:8 (NKJV) where Jesus says, "These people draw near to Me with their mouth, and honor Me with their lips, but their heart is far from me." To serve and even honor God goes beyond our mouth. Discipleship inevitably translates into action or a discipline to love one another, serve others, give, and even lead in our homes. However, it is vital to take into account that here, Jesus is not referring to the heart as the muscle in the center of our chest. He is alluding to the *mind or attitude* these types of people have in attempting to follow Him.

You must have an attitude to be willing to follow in faith. I can assure you, Simon and Andrew, as entrepreneurs, had a type of attitude to leave behind their successful family fishing business to follow a man they barely knew. I do not know many people today that would have done that. Nonetheless, it amazes me that in every sector or avenue where a man may find himself, his *attitude* or *thinking* is highly esteemed. His attitude or thinking are like trophies or badges of honor to let the world know where he stands corporately, economically, socially, or even politically. Ultimately, what makes a man a man is his *thinking*. What makes you think that it would be any different in the kingdom of God? Proverbs 23:7 (NKJV) says, "For as he thinks in his heart, so is he." Your life is the absolute projection of how or what you think.

God's Thoughts Expressed unto Man

To be a disciple requires the same thinking as the teacher or leader, which is why God considered it appropriate to give us His mind through His Word. The word of God is the mind of God given to man to follow; God's thoughts being revealed unto man. Simply amazing. I mean, that alone is enough to begin worshipping Him right now. Philippians 2:5 (NKJV) tells us, "Let this mind be in you that was also in Christ Jesus." A true disciple inherits the very expression of God's thoughts into a lifestyle that honors discipline. In other words, the individual is led by this *type of thinking* which was also in Jesus.

If we could take a moment to reflect on the distractions in our world, it is easy to be bombarded by the *thoughts* that emanate from the various types of mediums at our leisure. (e.g., tv, smartphones, social media, etc.) Your responsibility as priests requires you to have a well-balanced life that allows you to be "in the world, but not of it." Meaning, you take time in your 24-hour day schedule to spend time with God by reading the Word of God (His thoughts), meditating on the Word of God (His thoughts), then declaring the Word of God (His thoughts). Now, this may start as a routine, but with discipline will become a way of life.

You, one who is *fearfully and wonderfully made, God's chosen ones, and created after the likeness of God,* your thoughts keep you in a suitable posture for learning, maturing, and even correction. As a child grows, learns, and inherits a *way of thinking,* the parent applies the correction. So, Proverbs 3:12 (NKJV) tells us, "For whom the Lord loves He corrects, just as a father the son in whom he delights.

Often correction for men is an area that is less tolerable due to the natural tendency to want to oppose any person who is of authority. To refrain from *the correction* of any authoritative figure such as an officer, pastor, boss, manager, or even politician is to disregard God's hand of discipline. In Romans 13:1—2 (NKJV), it says, "Let every soul be subject to the governing authorities. For there is no authority except from God, and God appoints the authorities that exist. Therefore, whoever resists the authority resists the ordinance of God, and those who resist will bring judgment on themselves." As it relates to Christendom, if you are not willing to be corrected in any way, not only are you disqualified, but you are also incapable of *following* God.

Take an Account

As I expressed earlier in this chapter, fulfilling the priestly duties of your household is an ongoing process. Let me be the first to tell you. Again, this is a task that cannot be fulfilled through osmosis. It requires discipline and an initiative to take up the mandate with great honor. In my household, one of the weaknesses I had coming into the marriage was the capacity to manage. Have you ever had the feeling of just stuff slipping through your hands? I had issues managing my time and finances, but most importantly, time would reveal my wife's needs and emotions to a certain degree.

Now, I do not believe no one wakes up and decides to mismanage their assets or anything that they have deemed as valuable, for that matter. In my opinion, self-reflection and even open dialogue with your spouse is essential for success in this area. Before I attempt to go down this path, under no conditions am I suggesting the husband is responsible for every aspect of his home, for the philosophy is simply unbiblical. Proverbs 31:27 (NKJV) tells us that a godly wife "watches over the ways of her household and does not eat the bread of idleness." There is a partnership in building a Godly home. So, relax, fellas; you are not expected to *lift the entire burden of the household on your own*; however, you are to take inventory or an account of what comes into your home, which is essential in keeping order.

If we would look in 2 Kings 12:4 (NKJV), it says, "And Jehoash said to the priests, "All the money of the dedicated gifts that are brought into the house of the Lord, each man's census money, each man's assessment money, and all the money that a man purposes in his heart to bring into the house of the Lord." So King Jehoash gives the priests the responsibility of taking an account or collecting anything of value, anything of significant worth that would enter through the doors of the house of Lord. The priests, in principle, had an eye out for anything of value. They were the first to touch what was precious as it entered the temple's gates; and the last to secure it in a safe place, such as in the treasure room.

When taking inventory of your household, you as a priest must first carefully assess everything that enters through the front door of your home. One of the greatest countermeasures in protecting your household is through *awareness*. This initiative creates in you and me a *posture of attention*. It will afford us to have a grasp of the trajectory of our household's affairs. This idea consists of the bills the two of you receive, tax notices, doctor appointments, invitations of special engagements, and even guests you allow to visit. You may now be thinking, "Is this important to my marriage?" The answer is: "Most certainly." There is nothing more frustrating to a wife during a time of strategizing and planning than for her to ask the husband questions like: "Well, what do you think?" "What should we do?" and "Do you think we should?" and you do not have a response.

All I can tell you, do not expect to sleep in the same bed with your spouse that evening. Expect a rough night on the couch.

Though this task could be difficult, deciding to be well-informed of your household affairs helps you carry out your priestly role and creates an open conversation space with you and your spouse. Furthermore, when both husband and wife know what enters their doors, the *power of agreement* is more likely to be obtained.

For instance, should my wife ask me a question regarding a financial decision, having a voice or suggestion pertinent to her question, in theory, gives her something to consider. Now, contingent on the conversation that follows, we can then enter into prayer if we agree. Matthew 18:19 (NKJV) states, "Again I say to you that if two of you agree on earth concerning anything that they ask, it shall be done for them by My Father who is in heaven." This scripture echoes the power of God operating efficiently within a marriage.

"Like-Mind Connection" Wrap-Up:

1. Are there any areas of progress in your life that you have deliberately forfeited? If so, what is your plan of action to recover that place of victory?
2. Where is your level of discipline as it relates to being a disciple of Jesus?
3. Is management an area of weakness or strength? If a weakness, in what ways are you working with your spouse to improve?

The Respect for Finances

*"You must gain control over your money, or
the lack of it will forever control you."*

~ DAVE RAMSEY

If truth be told, finances could singly be the number one thought
on millions of people's minds daily, especially here in the United
States. Allocating our income towards bills, car maintenance, kid's
college tuition, personal needs, daycare, etc., requires planning to
ensure life as a manager of finances isn't a balancing act across a
tight rope but rather a firm walk at a constant pace. Now, consider
the thought of two people coming together to share that same
responsibility and burden of managing their finances. As you would
imagine, this requires the couple to be disciplined and *flow together*
as it relates to the management of financial affairs.

Nearly every sector of society (e.g., politics, agriculture,
manufacturing, etc.) is impacted to the degree of how well or how
poorly finances are managed. Do you want proof? As of this book
writing, the U.S. is now in debt by over $22.7 trillion; this number
is steadily increasing. (U.S. National Debt Hits Record $22 Trillion,
2019. Feb 13.) Make no mistake about it; our nation has turned a

blind eye to the mismanagement of this financial epidemic and is now stuck in the quicksand of overindulgence.

The Kingdom of Heaven is Like

Unlike our nation, thankfully, the Kingdom of Heaven is not in debt, nor is there lack or poverty. To bring context, the Kingdom of Heaven is the inauguration of the new covenant here on Earth; it is the operation of heaven. I like to describe it as *the how-to operate* while living here on earth. That is right; God desires the *earth to operate as it is in heaven*, as Matthew 6:10 – NKJV tells us.

The book of Matthew, which is considered a kingdom book, tells us in chapter 13 verse 31 (NKJV), "The kingdom of heaven is like a mustard seed, which a man took and sowed in his field." It is critical to hear and note the operation here: *took and sowed in his field*. In the Kingdom of Heaven, there is a way finances are handled and managed which is nothing like how the world *manages* its money. The Kingdom of Heaven operates by the *principle of sowing seed to gain a harvest, while the world's system operates by indulging the seed in gaining leverage.* One may be thinking: "So, are you suggesting I should just sow my entire income to gain a return potentially?" Well, of course not. Doing so would be unwise and unbiblical, but as a single, especially as a married couple, you must first view finances as a *slave to you and not the other way around*. Still, to see it as such, you and I must first know Who it belongs to moving forward.

To One He Gave

To attempt to address this matter, in Matthew's Gospel, Jesus begins to tell his disciples about the parable of talents found in

Matthew 25:14—30 (NKJV), in which a master went on a long journey and entrusted his property to his three servants. The Bible mentions in Matthew 25:15 (NKJV), "To one he gave five talents, to another two, to another one, each according to his ability." When the master finally returned from his long trip, he began to assess how well they managed the talents given to them. As a result, two of the three servants multiplied what was provided. In Matthew 25:21 (NKJV), the master says to them, "Well done, good and faithful servant. You were faithful over a few things; I will make you ruler over many things. Enter in the joy of your lord."

Can you imagine the feeling of accomplishment these two servants must have felt hearing this kind of reverence from their master? It is the "ol atta boy" word of affirmation that only a loving father would give his son to acknowledge his success. Concerning the last servant, scripture reveals that he buried his talents in the ground, in the same property entrusted to him. He then gave all the excuses for why he chose not to multiply what was provided. Wow, it sounds like someone did not get the memo. The master replies in Matthew 25:26 (NKJV), "You wicked and slothful servant!" Ouch! What a solid and direct statement. You can hear the tension in this moment of confrontation. The master later tells this servant in Matthew 25:27 (NKJV), "So you ought to have deposited my money with the bankers, and at my coming, I would have received back my own with interest."

Entrusted Responsibility

This parable, in my opinion, alludes to how we are only stewards of what God entrusts to us. Make no mistake about it; everything we earn monetarily is from God our Father. As believers of the kingdom faith, you and I must have respect and accountability for managing and planning our daily affairs. Anyone entrusted with some property then takes on the role of stewardship over what was given to them. They are not owners, yet they have the responsibility to manage what has been given.

Has it ever dawned on you that you and I do not necessarily *own* our earned wages, inheritance, stock investments, or settlements? To suggest we *own* our money is to adopt the belief that you and I are its creator or origin. Psalms 24:1(NKJV) tells us, "The earth is the Lord's, and all its fullness, the world and those who dwell therein."

To further help me drive this point, the economy was solely based on agriculture and healthy livestock one had in their possession in biblical times. The livestock especially was considered units of currency, in which an individual could exchange for other goods or even property for that matter. Psalms 50:10 (NKJV) then pick up from where Psalms 24:1 (NKJV) left off and tells us, "For every beast of the forest is Mine, and the cattle on a thousand hills." If that's not God's seal of ownership, I am not sure what else is. But, again, this denotes that God the Father, as rightful Owner or Creator of money, has given us stewardship of His creation. So, in all actuality, your *happiness* or the euphoric feeling you experience when your finances seem to be *smiling back at you* is contingent on how well you, the steward, can manage what you have in your possession.

I Need Help

When Tanisha and I began dating, over time, another weak trait of mine became exposed. I was negligent and maybe even ignorant in handling my financial affairs. On one occasion, she noticed on the kitchen counter of my apartment piles; I mean piles of unopened mail from bill collectors. My thinking then: "Out of sight, out of mind." I can recall her asking me, "Why haven't you opened your mail?" "Great question," I thought. My ego would not disclose the mere fact that I did not trust myself to handle finances considering all the wrong choices in my past. Experiencing car repossession, massive credit card debt, and constantly scraping by until my next paycheck, the fear of the thought of having to tell a debtor, "I do not have it," seem to float around in my head like a bubble that refuses to pop. Here is the eye-opener: I was a Christian who loved Jesus. Someone who faithfully tithed. Someone who sowed and gave. But I was deep in debt, still broke, and could not handle my financial affairs. I knew I was not living the *more abundant life* the Bible speaks on. So here is one of the most challenging and most prominent lessons I learned in my walk with Christ: "Until I respect God's finances, it will not in return respect me." What was lacking for me concerning the area of money was wisdom.

One common thread many *Christians* have is working a principle but lack the wisdom to know when or how to apply the principle in the arena of faith. According to Proverbs 4:7 (NKJV), "Wisdom is the principle thing; therefore get wisdom. And in all your getting, get understanding." The inability to utilize both creates frustration, a poverty mindset, and what I struggled with, even insecurities. Ultimately, you will begin to doubt yourself in the areas where faith should be operating at its highest. For you and me, this explains why wisdom is so important. James 1:5 (NKJV) tells us, "If any of you lacks wisdom, let him ask of God, who gives to all liberally and without reproach, and it will be given to him."

To highlight the significance of wisdom concerning the *arena of finances* in my life, even though I stubbornly insisted on doing things my way, He still had a peculiar way of reaching me. I can assure you; this gracious act was only by the mercy of God. I love how Proverbs: 1:20—22 (NKJV) puts it, "Wisdom calls aloud outside; she raises her voice in the open squares. She cries out in the chief concourses; At the openings of the gate in the city, she speaks her words: "How long, you simple ones, will you love simplicity? For scorners delight in their scorning, and fools hate knowledge?" Friend, let me be real clear; it is not in God's will for no man to lack any good thing. Unfortunately, due to my years of ignorance, I fell waist-deep into financial despair. Thank God my wife was the *voice of wisdom* that assisted me in becoming a better manager of finances. Because of her spiritual gift of wisdom, I eradicated a significant amount of my debt during that time.

As expected, in marriage, where one lacks in a particular area, their spouse comes along to help balance the boat, not to rock it. In the area of finances, I would describe myself as a giver. Make no doubt about it, my wife can attest. It brings me great joy to see someone benefit from what God allowed to flow from my hands and into theirs. Nonetheless, on the other hand, my wife does not necessarily have that same gift as I do; as I alluded to earlier, she operates in the spiritual gift of wisdom. Thank God. Understand, Tanisha was not necessarily a tither or sower in the *traditional sense.* Not that she did not believe in the biblical principle on sowing and tithing, it was that she needed what she was to me in the area of finances: *assistance.* Who better to assist her than me, her husband, who operates in this spiritual gift? She also became faithful in this area through her observation of my faithfulness and her own time with God.

Now, of course, I would love to depict a perfect framed picture that this was a smooth transition without any disagreements and *little leprechauns rode on magic unicorns throughout our home.* Still, this adjustment was something we both had to work through together in conversation and prayer. Not only did we have to *accept* each other's gift, but we each also had to go a step further in *honoring* each other's gift. Here is why: For us, our marriage hinged upon these two spiritual gifts for stability. Together, I can honestly say, they have saved our marriage from "piercing ourselves through with many sorrows," as 1 Timothy 6:10 (NKJV) indicates. Simply put, we chose not to fight against what honors us.

Finances are more of a spiritual element than a physical one. For instance, we all know how money makes us feel when we have it and when we don't. Our entire countenance changes, even down to our walk. Which explains why we as God's children must have authority over it at all *costs*—pun intended. If this is our stance and belief, you and I must tell our finances where it will go, what it will do, and how our household should benefit from it. Yes, that is right; *how our household should benefit from it.* I like what Ecclesiastes 7:12 (NKJV) tells us about money. It says, "For wisdom is a defense as money is a defense, but the excellence of knowledge is that wisdom gives life to those who have it." Did you see that? Finances only mimic what is planned accordingly by wisdom. I will attempt to put it another way; money is only as adequate as the wisdom behind it—this is a game-changer. Wisdom has been around even before the foundations of the world. Like wisdom, our finances' overall plan is to protect our household. Think of it like this, your finances now become a *defensive team player* for you. As you run the plays, you expect to witness your finances demonstrate what was agreed on in the *marital team huddle.*

Within the Huddle

The dilemma within most *marital team huddles*, you will often find disagreements, resentment, selfishness, and countless conflicts concerning finances. Our adversary, Satan, knows this and will do anything to cause confusion and discontentment in finances, especially in a marriage. One of the most significant agreements my wife and I had coming into our marriage was the idea that all the money that entered our home is *our money.* Being *like-minded* in that area abandoned the *separate but equal* mentality and cultivated a *better-together attitude* moving forward. Here was our rationale: "Why become the thorn in our side when we can simply be the solution?" We had an understanding that should I get a raise, she then gets a raise. So, in turn, our home gets a raise. Should she get a promotion, I then get a promotion; our home gets a promotion. Get the idea?

When words like *ours* morph into words like *yours* or *mine* between husband and wife, it constitutes division not only in marriage, planning but ultimately in the home. As Mark 3:25

(NKJV) states, "And if a house is divided against itself, that house cannot stand." I repeat, money is only as effective as the wisdom behind it. When there is no wisdom within the huddle of strategizing and planning, finances can't carry out the mission it was purposed to do; that is to protect. What good is protection when it is not active or even present? Without this protection, as one can imagine, it would be pretty challenging to live a normal life due to the amount of exposure.

The Vulnerable Life

No one likes to feel vulnerable; it is a component of human nature grafted into the core of who we all are. To be vulnerable denotes exposure from outside influences and elements that may cause harm or damage to what you and I deem valuable. If you think about it, naturally, every decision you and I make concerning our finances somehow relates to the level of exposure we attempt to avoid. So, for example, we only budget our finances, so the money we earn or receive is appropriately allocated to our daily obligations.

Studies have shown that the number one reason for arguments amongst married couples is money. Why? Think of it like this; imagine you have a couple who uses their finances as a literal shield to protect their household. The two must walk simultaneously for their *shield* to work efficiently against the onslaught of attacks. Should one get out of sync or move too far left when one moves slightly right due to miscues, arrows from the outside are more likely to hit vulnerable *targets* on the inside.

Here's what you and I must know, the very moment the house takes a causality in the form of a devastating foreclosure, repossession, or bankruptcy, often there is blame or fault towards one or the other, which creates derision within the home. As a result, the trust in the marriage has been sabotaged. Satan now uses this wedge to create a tug-of-war competition between spouses with the same *shield* intended to keep him out. For instance, when one spouse wants to use the extra money for a much-needed vacation or a new vehicle purchase, the other wants to use it to close the exposure created from previous bad decisions. As you would imagine, these "little foxes" destroy marriages as quickly as they both say, "I do" at the altar.

For Better or for Worse

Studies have proven that, on average, couples that have significant disagreements about their finances at least once a week are 30 more times likely to get a divorce. (Divorce Statistics: Over 115 Studies, Facts and Rates for 2020, 2020.) This statistic should confirm that love is not the only thing that keeps a man and woman happily married. If we can be transparent, the love the two have for one another will not necessarily keep the lights on, put food on the table, nor gas in the tank. Unfortunately, most marriages today seldomly are not prepared for the actual "better or for worse." Based on the statistic given earlier, it is apparent that finances have a significant role in the rate of divorce in our country.

The Breadwinner?

What first comes to mind when you hear the word "breadwinner?" This word often denotes an individual who is the primary source of income of their family. So be that husband or wife, they have taken on the role as the individual who earns income that suffices their overall household expenses. If you were born in either the Baby Boomer or Generation X era, traditionally, the husband *brings home the bacon* while the wife is the *homemaker*. During the mid- 1950s up to around the late 1960s, there would be popular tv family sitcoms, such as *The Honeymooners* and *Leave It to Beaver,* reflecting this idea that would ultimately be woven into the very fabric of the American culture we are now so accustomed to today.

Over the decades, society has evolved, and the number of women who have decided to enter the workforce increased exponentially. In contrast to the Baby Boomer era, more dual-income homes are now leading this charge due to that couple's unique sense of partnership. Of course, this does not necessarily mean a single-income home is at any disadvantage. Still, you and I should carefully consider that it is entirely up to that couple whether their home would become a single or a dual-income household in marriage.

Godliness Should Not Exempt Responsibility

Against popular belief, no scriptural references validate that the husband should be the home's breadwinner. However, earlier in this book, we have confirmed that husbands' role in marriage is to be the priest of their home. This role constitutes the husband becoming his wife's head as Christ is the head of the church, as Ephesians 5 (NKJV) speaks on. This headship or covering is unmistakably anointed to provide protection and identity for the wife within the marriage. So put, even if a husband is not necessarily the breadwinner of his home, this should not discredit his role as covering for his wife due to either agreement or unforeseen financial circumstances.

To be transparent, since being married, I, unfortunately, have experienced two major unforeseen job layoffs, and Tanisha temporarily became the sole earner in our household. However, this did not disqualify my role nor the responsibility that I had as a husband. By the grace of God, I still managed to provide other essential needs for my wife and our household as the head.

Concerning men entitled as *breadwinners,* one scripture I believe is often misinterpreted to support this belief is 1 Timothy 5:8 (NKJV). It says, "But if anyone does not provide for his own, and especially for those of his household, he has denied the faith and is worse than an unbeliever." First, I think it is necessary to point out that 1 Timothy is a book that focuses on what godliness should resemble in the house of God. Paul, an apostle and church leader, is writing to a young Timothy, his protégé in Ephesus, attempting to address honoring widows and the elders in the church. We can only assume that the church of the Ephesus congregation consisted of widows and the elderly. For context, Paul essentially instructs Timothy that *anyone* who claimed to be of the faith should provide care and other necessities to anyone of their own family or household. In other words, the principle we need to capture here is that no matter the gender, you take care of your family when they are in need or destitute. This mandate from Paul is a call for men of the faith, as it is for women to exemplify excellence. 1 Timothy 5:16 (NKJV) says, "If any believing man or woman has widows, let them relieve them, and do not let the church be burdened, that it may relieve those who are widows." Paul unapologetically addresses the church of Ephesus, by way of his spiritual son Timothy, that godliness should never exempt responsibility.

"Like-Mind Connection" Wrap-Up:

1. Do you and your spouse view your finances as a *defensive team player* within your home?
2. Do you and your spouse have an active strategy of how your money should work for you?
3. Are tithing and sowing a biblical principle you and your spouse believe in and honor? If not, why?

When the Bottom Falls Out

"The experience of democracy is like the experience of life itself—always changing, infinite in its variety, sometimes turbulent and all the more valuable for having been tested by adversity."
~ JIMMY CARTER

Besides witnessing my children enter this world, marrying the love of my life in August of 2013 in Raleigh, NC, was the happiest and most fulfilling day of my life. That day, I remember standing at the altar, thinking to myself, "Am I dreaming?" "Is this real?" "Am I even ready to go through with this?" All kinds of random thoughts are flooding my mind. Of course, I am getting ready to step into a new place in life I have never been before. Undoubtedly, we were both on the cusp of our own *moon landing experience* right here on earth, at one particular moment in time.

In Raleigh's most elegant wedding venues, I am looking miles on end over the capital city on the 28th floor, in a sky ballroom of the City Club of Raleigh. I am, accompanied by my dad as my best man and my mother sitting in the front row. Off to my left, my younger and older brother, my best friend, and my future brother-in-law as my groomsmen. There in the center, my pastor is officiating the ceremony. Loved ones and friends all smiling and tearing up, all in anticipation of this union between man, woman, and God. I am thinking, "Today is the day two lives will forever be changed, and I'm hoping for only the better."

The DJ begins to play our wedding song. I see my soon-to-be wife, accompanied by her father, graciously being escorted down the aisle. I am standing there in total amazement. I am blinking almost uncontrollably because the entire ballroom appears to be filling up with some *mysterious fog.* I am thinking to myself, "I do not recall discussing anything about smoke machines in the budget?" But no, there were no smoke machines at all. Later, Tanisha asked me, "Did you see all of the smoke that filled the room?" Thinking I was the only one that noticed, I replied, "You noticed too?! Yes, I thought my eyes were playing tricks on me." Accepting what only the two of us experienced together, we took it as God blessing our marriage by filling that room up with His glory. Yes, a match created in heaven, manifested right here on earth.

Our pastor began his opening words as tradition goes, followed by my wife's father giving her away—the exchange of rings. To be honest, at that moment, I was desperately trying not to forget her left hand from her right. Everything was such a blur at that moment. But it was only until our pastor eloquently and beautifully began to define what marriage is in the sight of God and why marriage is so sacred to Him that it grabbed our hearts. His delivery resonated with the two of us so profoundly that strangely somewhere in us, we both knew to comprehend what was addressed first required us to live out. What was spoken before an attendance of over 100 people that day not only needed to be addressed to singles and married couples but, most importantly, as my wife and I will one day soon see, prophetically our lives. Who knew within a few months from that day that both of our faith would be tested tremendously? Leaving that place of glory, the top floor of one of the tallest buildings in the city, to experiencing the "shadows of death" at ground zero was a free-fall neither of us ever expected. But, I guess in God's mysterious way, our *free-fall together* would be necessary in how we would *rebuild from a place of ruin.*

Fire Duty Calls

You might recall earlier in this book of me mentioning that I worked for a reputable international IT company, in which I worked a grueling 12-hour nightshift. The company immediately reported a massive lay-off in my region, and unfortunately, many of my colleagues were let go. But to be transparent, I was never happier for the chance of being allowed to go at that time. I took it as my departure. I knew this would grant me more time to spend with family and give me a fresh start to re-gather and re-focus on what I wanted to do in the IT profession.

That night as I made my way into the building, unsurprisingly, no more than an hour later, I was called into my manager's office to be informed that I was *being let go*. I remember him saying these words to me: "I have been on fire duty all day, and your name is on the list." I was given my severance package and signed additional forms to what seemed to be of no end. Because integrity plays a vital role in my life, I worked that night shift; not surprisingly, in great spirits. The following morning, I was escorted out of the front door with a new lease on life. As a newlywed, of course, I began to think about all the *what-ifs* concerning the future. My wife told me she had never seen anyone that happy in being let go from their job. But, even then, I just knew God had so much in store for me as an individual, and I was ready to walk with Him on the journey, or at least I thought I was.

My wife was entering law school at North Carolina Central University, and at the time, we were living off my severance pay from my former employer. We managed to stay afloat, but as you know that money does not last forever. So, I decided to apply for unemployment, which of course, I ran into a discrepancy with the Division of Employment Security of NC. Sad to say, I did not receive any benefits for nearly seven months while I was unemployed. Down to a couple of hundreds in the bank, what would we do? Naturally, pressure began to grip its coils around me. We needed income and FAST!

When Reality Meets Spirituality

In the midst of what was going on under our roof that early October, I received a phone call from my older brother that our beloved mother was rushed to Wake Forest Baptist Medical Center in Winston Salem, NC, and admitted to ICU. "What?! What could be going on?" I thought. My wife and I drove to Winston-Salem, NC, not knowing what to expect. When we arrived at the hospital, my stomach and legs felt as if they were no longer part of my anatomy. I can recall my legs shaking uncontrollably, not knowing what to expect. I saw my mother lying there, seemingly unresponsive, with a trach in her throat as I entered the ICU. I see my dad walking down the hallway to us; he then tells me, "Your mom is sick, Jules; she has ALS." I'm thinking, "What is that? Of course, there must be some treatment, right?" Later, I found out that what is also known as Lou Gehrig's disease has no treatment or cure. To add insult to injury, our parents kept this secret from my brothers and me for months. As years have gone by, I now understand why they both chose not to disclose my mother's diagnosis, but I admit, at that time, I was just angry and did not want to hear it.

With only she and I in the room, I slowly sat down in a chair positioned at the foot of my mother's bed, looking at her while she was in some medicated coma-like state, and softly I said to myself, "Am I going to lose my mom?" Somewhere in me, I expected God to answer right at that very moment. But, instead, all I heard was the constant beeping of the monitors in the room. For the first time in my life, here is where my reality collided with my faith head-on. At this very moment, I am attempting to grasp and internalize what is being presented right before my very eyes. The reality is that my mom is battling for her life, while my faith is telling me, "God is a healer." Worlds apart, I seem to find myself tightly stretched thin by the two dimensions.

Stepping into the Ring

I am in a strange place now. I would love to tell you that my faith rose to the occasion unwavering in this place where I was presented with hopelessness; the truth of the matter is that it became timid. As statistics would prove, and as far as I knew, ALS had no losing record. At that time, my faith was too reluctant to step into the ring against an opponent who never lost. So much for my opportunity to re-enact a *David and Goliath-like victory story,* I thought.

Nevertheless, here is the power of marriage: What I initially presumed was *my fight,* my wife graciously reminded me that it *was ours.* Rest assured that at that moment, Ecclesiastes 4:9—10 (NKJV) where it tells us, "Two are better than one because they have a good reward for their labor. For if they fall, one will lift up his companion." took on a whole different meaning to me. It became my *word of life.* My wife's encouragement, strength, and faith in the God in me provoked me into stepping into that ring with confidence, not only with the confidence I needed but with a renewed perspective that she accompanies me.

Months would go by; my mom was continually being readmitted to the hospital until she just wanted to remain at home to be comfortable as much as possible. Now in great expectation, passion, and faith, I continued praying for her healing, telling her, "Mom, you are going to beat this!" There was nothing in me that told me otherwise. But, unfortunately, noticing her lose weight, unable to speak due to the symptoms of the disease, not seeing the results

I desired, as you would imagine, my faith became bruised and frustrated. It would only be around Christmas of that year that I would soon realize why.

Praying Against an Answered Prayer

As Christmas was fast approaching in 2013, Ryan, my younger brother, mentioned to us later that he asked our mother what she wanted for Christmas, her reply, "A new body." Did you get that? What faith! Even in what she knew could be her last days, the *confidence in her* groaned for the redemption of her body, as Romans 8:23 (NKJV) tells us. The truth of the matter is that my mother wanted to go home to be with the Lord. She knew that "absent from the body is to be present with the Lord," as 2 Corinthians 5:8 (NKJV) references. So, though she loved her family with all of her heart, she began making the necessary final preparations with my father for her departure. She was at peace. Who am I or anyone, for that matter, to pray against an answered prayer? As the family would all learn years later, it was by her departure that my entire immediate family either: *gave their life to the Lord, rededicated their life to the Lord, or strengthened their faith in the Lord.* Jesus says it like this in John 12:24 (NKJV), "Most assuredly, I say to you unless a grain of wheat falls into the ground and dies, it remains alone; but if it dies, it produces much grain." Yes, this woman was ready to produce much grain.

The Call

Early morning of May 1, 2014, I received the call that would forever alter our lives, marriage, and even how we viewed our faith in God. Roughly around 3 am, my dad calls me. Looking at the phone for a few seconds, bracing for what I would hear on the other side of the phone; my wife has her hand on my back for extra needed support. I pick up. As expected, crying hysterically, I hear my dad saying, "She's gone! ... She's gone!" In a moment, what I thought would be a feeling of sadness, was a total sigh of relief. There was a feeling of comfort for my mother, who suffered those grueling and uncomfortable months, also a relief of mere dread of never knowing when I was going to receive this call. As we began to make our way to my parent's house, all the emotions associated with loss began to surface. In the days and months that would follow, life seemed to have tested everything I ever knew of God, my faith, role as a husband; yet I never questioned Him. At 29, I lost the first love of my life, the one who knew me more than anyone on this earth. My mother was gone.

New Normal

Life was still waiting for us after laying our mother to rest. We reluctantly had to accept our reality, our *new normal.* I believe that this is what Paul refers to in Philippians 4:11 (NKJV) "I learned in whatever state I am, to be content" With new seasons, requires the ability to adapt. We may not necessarily know or even care, for that matter, about the reasons behind *winter,* but in time you will have to be content with that season's overall purpose. In the spiritual, contentment can accept a given circumstance solely based on God's sovereignty, not by human preference. Let me put it like this: Moving to Florida, *the Sunshine State,* to embrace the resort-life living during this time would not permit us from escaping the harsh reality of *our* winter. You know as well as I do, growth does not take place on the run but only within the will of God. Now, this definition of contentment may sound comprehendible, but I can assure you it was not the most straightforward principle for me to live out, as you soon will learn.

I am unemployed and looking for work, trying to be everything I know how to be to my wife, wrestling with the grief of the loss of my mother, and my bank account gradually getting lower; I admit I fell into a deep state of depression. I can assure you; this is nowhere for anyone to become comfortable. Numb to life, numb to my responsibilities, numb to my church, numb to my wife, and even numb to God. I was angry and blamed God for everything. I mean, everything. There was a strong resentment towards God, and honestly, I felt as if I could not correct it, even though I knew I was the one in error. During these pressing months, I carelessly allowed Satan to enter my marriage like some viral infectious disease. Mentally, I had gone into autopilot, not necessarily concerned about where my mind drifted off to or even the ramifications. Proverbs 6:27 (NKJV) tells us, "Can a man take fire in his bosom, and his clothes not be burned?" You bet; I had all the matches at my disposal, and boy was I going to burn, and everything I once deemed valuable would suffocate in the smoke. Again, as I articulated earlier in this book, when the husband is physically, mentally, or spiritually absent, he essentially leaves his wife exposed to every fiery dart from the adversary. *He is her protection, head, covering* as Ephesians 5:23 (NKJV) references. Wives, when your *head* is not in the game, expect a deficit.

There were two doors I knew I could re-open to escape this new reality. Ironically, I felt the world's system might not have been the overall solution, but it could at least *assist* me momentarily. Behind door #1 was alcohol, which I never had a genuine taste for even in my earlier days, but I was addicted to the state it put me mentally, of course. It was a form of escapism. Unfortunately, it was not free. You know that. The tradeoff for me just was not logical. Behind door #2 was pornography: every man's temptation; in which it was convenient, unnoticed, but most importantly; you guessed it, free. I chose door #2 as the *device* Satan would bound me by in my rebellion. As a result, I began to distance myself from my wife and even her affection. The intimacy I once had for her became tainted.

Increasingly, I found her to be my foe, instead of seeing her as my "good thing" according to Proverbs 18:22 (NKJV), "He who finds a wife finds a good thing."

The enemy even had me believe that my wife restricted me from seeing my mother as often as I would have liked to in the last months leading up to her departure. Secretly, I resented her for that. To add fuel to the fire, her mother was still healthy, living, and vibrant. This fact was a constant reminder of my loss. This resentment fueled many of our arguments; storming out of the house and driving to destinations that did not exist after a big argument was simply the fruit of my selfish and rebellious behavior. Just driving around to escape became more and more frequent for me. The truth of the matter, I no longer cared. I was a man on the run. During this tumultuous time, the same mouth I once used to build and speak life into people, I used to attack, belittle, and tear down my wife. Verbal abuse was my weapon of choice. I essentially became a monster who hated his reflection and the affliction I knew I was causing, but how do I stop it? I constantly had thoughts circling in my head like: "Who is this person I now see in the mirror?" "Where did he come from?" and "How did I end up here?" These were the honest questions I needed to answer myself. Thank God for grace.

For me, it was either run back to the Father in humility or continue to run from Him in my resentment. I admit, running from Him became too exhausting for me. I needed rest. The kind of rest Jesus refers to in Matthew 11:29 (NKJV), "and you will find rest for your souls." Around this time, I recall a song that would often play on the local gospel radio station by Kevin Levar called "A Heart that Forgives." In our apartment, sitting on the side of the tub in our bathroom, words from that song began to come to mind. Tears began to flow from my eyes uncontrollably.

I began to repent to God for having resentment and anger towards Him for so long. Not only that, but I also had to repent for having the same level of hatred towards my wife. My ignorance essentially caused conflict within a covenant I vowed to protect in the sight of God. I was so ashamed of myself. Yet, right there in that bathroom, amid me worshipping, I felt my heart no longer confined and chained to a cell of bondage. The Father welcomed me back into His arms. I was once lost in my grief, sin, and anger, but I became aware of God's presence again in an instance—I was found.

Rebuilding the Wall

In the Bible, one of the most significant turning points recorded in history was when Babylon, a mighty kingdom ruled by Nebuchadnezzar II, conquered Jerusalem in approximately 587 BC. By breaking through Jerusalem's walls, his kingdom ultimately destroyed the city, leaving it in utter ruin and ashes. Soon after, King Nebuchadnezzar II and his troops led many citizens of Jerusalem into Babylon's captivity, leaving only a remnant behind.

Over 100 years would have gone by, and during that time, King Artaxerxes would rule Persia. His cupbearer, named Nehemiah (does the name sound familiar?), *learns that the walls of his ancestor's city, the great Jerusalem, still lie in total ruin.* Nehemiah is so devastated by this news that it brings him to mourning, fasting, and prayer. Nevertheless, God gives Nehemiah favor before the king, so he requests to travel to Jerusalem to *rebuild it.* King Artaxerxes not only gives Nehemiah permission to go to the city, but he also gives him all the materials he would need. Why is this short history lesson so important? Ultimately, Jerusalem's sin and rebellion caused their people to be carried off in captivity and left their city to be plundered, left in destruction. *Boy, this sure does sound familiar.*

News Flash: *When there is an awareness of sin, it will eventually provoke one to go back or turn around to make right.* Essentially, this is what repentance is—going back, not to visit and wallow in sin, but to acknowledge it or confess it before God. *Nehemiah is symbolic of an entire nation whose heart lays open upon the altar of repentance in the presence of God.* To put it in perspective, my awareness of my sin led me back into the presence of the Lord. Ironically, the harder I thought I was running from God for months, I was running right into the Father's arms.

Again, godliness does not neglect responsibility. I had work to do. As did Nehemiah, I knew I had the same grace and favor to consistently *re-build a wall around my marriage,* even in the face of ashes and ruins. Building upon what used to be or what represents failure is no easy task. Believe me. It takes great effort to search for hope at *ground zero.* As you will soon learn, the adversary will stop at nothing to hinder a movement, a pulse, or a life. He sees progress as a threat to his kingdom. It would take over a year of sitting under the Word of God at church, fasting, praying, and becoming more spiritually disciplined for me to get into a place where I could forgive myself for the damage I caused to my marriage and home. I was then able to walk in a level of maturity in God that I had never experienced. Here is the caveat, though I was spiritually growing, there were indications that my wife and I were no longer on the same frequency. Do not misunderstand; I allowed the lust, rebellion, ignorance, and resentment to plague my marriage; so, I had the responsibility to answer each of them through the grace of Jesus.

One Stone at a Time

In time, I would be able to find employment. I took that as an indication of better days to come. Sleep came much easier for me during that time. Unfortunately, though our household and marriage were gaining traction towards financial stability, it was still severely vulnerable. Due to my reckless behavior for months, Tanisha struggled with what I allowed in the marriage. One day at work, I recall receiving an unexpected text message informing me that she had been dealing with lust for months.

This day was the first time she ever became this transparent in expressing these struggles with me. Everything in me wanted to hold her and let her know she was not in this alone. But instead, in a *roundabout way*, I told her that I dealt with it and how I overcame it. But, this news was ripping me apart inside because I knew I had a huge role to play in it, as this was the first time in our marriage that the two of us had ever discussed lust or pornography. The truth of the matter is that once you expose the enemy in an area of vulnerability in your life, he has nowhere to hide. He no longer has an influence. Revelations 12:11 (NKJV) let us know that we "overcame him by the blood of the Lamb, and by the word of their testimony."

I want to reiterate, Satan sees progress as a threat to his kingdom, especially in a marriage. While my wife and I prepared to make the necessary adjustments to improve our relationship, Satan would use the same tactic he used on me, on my wife: *rebellion*. Why? Not only did I subject my marriage to its influence, but rebellion is also essentially a by-product of pride, which in return kicked Lucifer (Satan) out of heaven. Isaiah 14:12—15 (NKJV) reads, "How you are fallen from heaven, O Lucifer, son of the morning! How you are cut down to the ground, you who weakened the nations! For you have said in your heart: "I will ascend into heaven, I will exalt my throne above the stars of God; I will also sit on the mount of the congregation on the farthest sides of the north; I will ascend above the heights of the clouds, I will be like the Most High." Yet you shall be brought down to Sheol, to the lowest depths of the Pit."

Seeing Through the Lens of Error

Rebellion inherently disrupts unity or the perfect and sovereign will of God. It only sees its plan through the *lens of error*. As the text indicates, rebellion (sin) has "weakened the nations" here on the earth. What better tactic to cause division than to inject this toxin into the heart of a child of God? As days would become weeks, weeks into months, my wife would begin to articulate that she was no longer *being fed* at the church we were attending. To hear that pierced through my heart like a knife. The last thing I ever wanted in our marriage was for one to grow and mature in our local church assembly and the other to become stagnant. What followed was my wife refusing to serve in any capacity as it related to the ministry. I knew it was simply too heavy of a burden to carry. Behind closed doors, there would be many reoccurrences of arguments and disagreements on this topic. The more and more she would bring this up, the closer I was to making the agonizing decision in uprooting and relocating to another church assembly.

I knew in my heart that should a man of God prematurely uproot himself from a place where he knows he is maturing (other than knowing God has called him to advance the kingdom in another geographical area), he puts his entire home in a posture of deficiency. This pattern I have seen all too often, of men uprooting from where God has planted him for a purpose that is far greater than himself. Involuntarily, I reasoned that to gain solace in my home, I was willing to uproot. Not because I wanted to, but for the sake of my marriage. I was willing to *die*.

On that following Sunday morning, I arose with a heavy heart. I knew that my ten-plus years of faithfully serving this church was coming to an end that day. The whole worship service for me personally was a blur. Everything seemed to move at such a slow pace—even words coming from the congregation's mouths. I was deeply saddened. As an attempt to hide my emotions, I did not want to speak to anyone. Although, after service, I attempted to find our Senior Pastor to get a brief meeting with him to tell him our decision, at that time, a visitor who attended our church that day wanted to speak with my wife and me directly. Surprisingly, she traveled from Virginia that Sunday.

I thought to myself, "This seems a bit odd." As she began to speak with us, she vividly began to tell us we were needed there and that God has unique plans for both of us. She even began to describe my *sacred place* in my home, where I have prayed the prayers for God to resolve this conflict within our marriage. Tanisha and I looked at each other in total amazement and just began to weep. "How could she have known?" There was absolutely *no way* she could have known this, other than by God sending her there that morning with this message, literally from the throne room of heaven as confirmation.

After speaking with her, my wife and I privately met with our Senior Pastor and Co-Pastor. After a heartfelt conversation with them and being ministered to, we all agreed that additional counseling in this phase of our marriage was very much needed. Through these sessions, healing, clarity, insight, and understanding were administered—this was the start of the two of us beginning the repair process and continuing to work on areas we *both* were in a deficit.

Building Blocks of Offense

As an addendum, there's no such thing as a perfect church. The church is not necessarily the fancy *brick and mortar*, rather the people who assemble. Anytime there are people, there will be moments of friction, annoyance, and frustration, which are fundamental building blocks of offense. Friend, this happens everywhere: on the job, in the line at the grocery store, in traffic (road rage), even within our own families.

I think Jesus was on to something, as He promised this would happen in Luke 17:1—3 (NKJV), "Then He said to the disciples, "It is impossible that no offenses should come, but woe to him through whom they do come! It would be better for him if a millstone were hung around his neck, and he were thrown into the sea than that he should offend one of these little ones. Take heed to yourselves. If your brother sins against you, rebuke him; and if he repents, forgive him." But here is the caveat, the offense will always be magnified through the *lenses of error.* It has become apparent this has become problematic in the traditional American church. Instead of being led by the Spirit in our decisions and actions, we mirror the world's way of reacting in the fashion that comes easiest to our flesh: *1. Leave the job. 2. Curse out the cashier at the grocery store. 3. Cut off the driver that cut us off two lights prior. 4. Refuse to participate in family reunions and festivities because of a particular family member. 5. Leave the church.* Inherently, what we allow to fester will gradually become our new normal, our world according to our eyes. Instead of addressing issues to get to the place of resolve, we would rather *nurse* them into a life of their own. In closing, you and I must address our problems at their *root* before we are tempted to partake of the *fruit* of bitterness, resentment, and unforgiveness.

"Like-Mind Connection" Wrap-up:

1. What are present and past failures within your marriage that have presented opportunities to rebuild? How was the overall process?
2. Is there anything too difficult to discuss with your spouse? If so, what ways could the two of you begin to build that bridge of communication?
3. Do you feel obligated to only repent to God and not to your spouse? Are there any exceptions?

Finding the Voice of
Your Marriage

*"How you use your voice is really important,
and it's really driven by context more than
anything else, and your tone of your voice will
immediately begin to impact somebody's mood
and immediately how their brain functions."*

~ CHRISTOPHER VOSS

O ne fascinating trait of a child who has yet to enter the world is the ability to learn from their surroundings. They come into the world ready to be impressed upon by their parents. Though they cannot talk, yet they have adopted a way to effectively communicate how they feel at any given moment: *crying.* Crying is the infant's natural way of letting their caregiver know that they are *hungry, sleepy, or uncomfortable.* Any parent will tell you, at first, this is a guessing game as it requires looking for context clues, such as a dirty diaper. "Oh, the horror!"

A newborn's learning ability allows them to pick up patterns of sounds, behaviors, gestures, and even the shape of lips or the mouth when an adult speaks to them. In no time at all, the newborn will begin to attempt to mimic and demonstrate what they hear, acclimating to the dynamics of the parent in a more direct and personable manner. As months go by and the infant becomes a toddler, as anticipated, the *cooing, grunts,* and *other adorable sounds* we parents have fallen in love with transitions into words. The exact words they may have learned underneath their parent's care. Our little bundle of joy now *has a voice*; this is a day of celebration for parents because there is no longer a guessing game in identifying a need. The child can directly voice their feelings. Despite this discovery, under the parent's *guidance and correction,* the child learns to articulate their feelings and evolve from them.

Lay of the Land

Moreover, this is the same approach any couple should take in preparing for pre-marital counseling, willing to be taught by a spiritual covering (e.g., Pastor or life coach*)* to find *their* voice within the perimeters of *their* marriage. Before many get married, they already have ideas on how it may be. The ideas stem from what they may have experienced or a memory of what marriage should be like living with their parents: some good behaviors, some bad. Approaching a new marriage based on the *lay of the land* of another marriage will not entirely benefit you in developing your voice in your marriage. If anything, it could harm it. For example, a child growing up and learning that to win a disagreement with his spouse, he would have to be more assertive and vocally overbearing to his significant other. Psychologically, to that child, the behavior could indicate a *voice* that communicates that the spouse is devalued, the spouse is disrespected, or the spouse is insignificant.

However, this could be conveyed differently to another child, contingent on that child's perception. As I mentioned prior, the dynamics of every marriage are different because not one person is the same. For instance, what may seem to come off as devaluing or disrespectful in one marriage may demonstrate qualities of assertiveness in another. Essentially, what works for one couple or individual, often will not work for another.

Please do not misunderstand; every newlywed, especially in their first year, are learning and will continue to do so throughout the marriage. Marriages naturally evolve as the people themselves evolve. However, what is acquired in pre-marital counseling is ultimately wisdom. Wisdom gives us the ability to discern, which will be required in the rough patches down the road. Proverbs 19:20 (NKJV) tells us, "Listen to counsel and receive instruction, that you may be wise in your latter days." In this safe setting of pre-marital counseling, what is administered to the man and woman is not opinionated suggestions given by man, rather Godly advice inspired by the Word of God.

Like my infant analogy, two people have come with the intent to receive, ready to listen. Their willingness to become vulnerable already puts them in a posture ready to receive instructions. The two have essentially begun developing their unique *voice* for their marriage by listening to wisdom inspired by the pure and unadulterated Word of God.

Where Are Your Expectations?

Pre-marital counseling should be an exciting time. In a private setting, you are learning on a deeper level how each other thinks, feels, and most importantly, you are learning one another's expectations within the marriage. Everyone has expectations. Expectations are predetermined ideas of what a person, place, or thing should be like or even do, given the *picture* created in their minds. Yet have you ever considered where exactly these ideas derived from and purpose? What is the motivation behind the *picture* we have created?

Placing marital expectations on a spouse is putting them at a disadvantage. Here is why: The moment an expectation is not fulfilled according to human standards, inevitably there are disappointments. One may be thinking, "Am I not supposed to expect the best from my spouse?" Not at all. There should be expectations concerning your marriage. However, exactly where we should place our expectation is the greater question we all need to consider.

I think Mark 10:17—23 (NKJV) projects this illustration in a way that challenges the human idea of where we often mistakenly place our expectations. For context, the scripture says:

"Now, as He was going out on the road, one came running, knelt before Him, and asked Him, "Good Teacher, what shall I do that I may inherit eternal life?" So, Jesus said to him, "Why do you call Me good? No one is good but One that is God. You know the commandments: 'Do not commit adultery, 'Do not murder,' 'Do not steal,' 'Do not bear false witness,' 'Do not defraud,' 'Honor your father and your mother.' And he answered and said to Him, "Teacher, all these things I have kept from my youth."

Then Jesus, looking at him, loved him, and said to him, "One thing you lack: Go your way, sell whatever you have and give to the poor, and you will have treasure in heaven; and come, take up the cross, and follow Me." But he was sad at this word and went away sorrowful, for he had great possessions. Then Jesus looked around and said to His disciples, "How hard is it for those who have riches to enter the Kingdom of God!"

It is very easy to be taken by surprise at Jesus' first response: "Why do you call Me good? No one is good but One, that is God." One may ask, "Why would Jesus ask this man such a direct question?" Well, first, we must understand that Jesus *is* the full expression of the true and living God. John 14:9 (NKJV), says "He who has seen Me has seen the Father," But what also needs to be considered here is that Jesus sees the heart of men. Jesus foreknew that within this man's heart lies the idea of *knowing the truth* was more appealing than *knowing the truth and following it.*

This guy had an erroneous belief system of what inheriting eternal life *must* be like: *easy*. Naturally, anything you and I associate with easy, painless, smooth, or straightforward is considered *good*. There is no cost. It is assumed that there is no sacrifice to be made. There will always be resistance when a *demand* is placed on the human heart that is not renewed in Christ Jesus. This principle applies to every aspect of our daily lives. To this man, what he learned through hear-say, provoked him to place his expectation on Someone Who is simply unaffiliated with *his* perception.

To go deeper, Jesus reveals to the reader a more profound issue going on internally with this man. We learn that this man's expectation solely resided in what was closest to his heart: *his possessions.* Scripture tells us that this man had "great possessions." Essentially, he was *married* to what he already invested his expectation in— *his possessions.*

Jesus addresses the man, "Why do you call Me good?" In other words, Jesus knew that once He did or said anything contrary to this man's expectation, He was no longer *good.* So Jesus puts it out there: "One thing you lack: Go your way, sell whatever you have and give to the poor, and you will have treasure in heaven; and come, take up the cross, and follow Me." Scripture goes on to let us know that the man was "sad at this word, and went away sorrowful, for he had great possessions." His perception of Jesus as the *Good Teacher* suddenly had to be *re-evaluated.*

How often have we consciously or even subconsciously treated our spouses as one of many possessions (e.g., house, car, bank account) and deposited all of our expectations on their shoulders for them to fulfill? Jesus makes this statement: "How hard is it for those who have riches to enter into the Kingdom of God?" This man struggled in *letting go* of what his heart has joined to—*his riches.* Mainly, Jesus highlights a principle: *Attempting to place expectations in anything other than the Father creates a stumbling block in return.*

But There is Hope

Another word for expectation is *hope*. According to the scripture, Romans 5:5 (NKJV) tells us, "Now hope does not disappoint, because the love of God has been poured out in our hearts by the Holy Spirit who was given to us." So, to clarify, the moment we place our hope (expectation) wholeheartedly into God as the head of our marriage, the Holy Spirit confirms it within our spirit, which registers with our souls that all is well. We learn this is the same *hope* we are saved in, according to scripture. It works identically with our salvation.

At the point of salvation, you and I confessed with our mouths that Jesus is Lord and believed in our hearts that God raised Him from the dead, according to Romans 10:9 (NKJV). You and I have never witnessed Jesus. We have never physically walked with Him nor talked with Him face-to-face. It would take *hope* to receive what has never been seen before. Romans 8:24 (NKJV) reads, "For we were saved in this hope, but hope that is seen is not hope; for why does one still hope for what he sees?" We received confirmation within our souls that "we were saved" by the Holy Spirit through our spirit.

I love how Hebrews 6:19 (NKJV) puts it, "This hope we have as an anchor of the soul, both sure and steadfast, and which enters the Presence behind the veil." No one can talk you out of your salvation when your soul is anchored in Jesus. So likewise, no one can persuade you out of a Godly marriage when your hope (expectation) rests in the God Who has ordained it. So, friend, when hope is appropriately placed, it leaves no room for disappointment.

Putting Everything on the Table

~~~~~~~~

I am not the biggest fan of surprises. For one, my reaction may not be what the other individual would have expected. Secondly, I simply do not like the *feeling* of being caught off guard. Ironically, I would prefer to give the surprises, which, as you might have guessed, may not come off as I would expect. Either way, we have all been on both sides of the spectrum; some good, some we would rather not mention again if the truth be told. In relationships, especially in marriage, concerns, issues, agendas, and even assumptions should all be *placed on the table* in the very beginning.

Here is why: Again, referring to the baby analogy from earlier, it takes the *assumptions* or *guessing* out of the scope of marriage as it concerns the direction or path the two have decided to move forward in. So far in my eight years of marriage, I have learned that anything you refuse to speak on, despite the reasons, will speak out for you later. Luke 8:17 (NKJV) tells us, "For nothing is secret that will not be revealed, nor anything hidden that will not be known and come to light."

To better illustrate, a few years ago, Tanisha and I befriended a newly engaged couple who seemed to be very enthusiastic about their new married life together. Who would not be? From the outside looking in, it appeared this couple had all the *building blocks* they would need to have an explementary marriage any single would admire, like the nice car, lovely apartment, great careers. Well, at least it appeared that way. One thing that seemed to be lacking was *communication*. During a couple's outing, they shared an area of struggle: transparency. We learned that the man acted out his daily routine for weeks and would be gone for eight hours of the day. His fiancé reasonably assumed he would work; however, he ultimately revealed that he had lost his job. Instead of sharing that he lost his job, he would have rather spent the day running errands and driving idly.

Somehow or another, he determined it would be better to conceal the truth rather than disclose it. Maybe his decision was dictated by fear: the feeling of failure, how his fiancé would view him, the image he would portray in sight of his future in-laws. Who knows? Instead of building trust, this couple was heading into the beginning of their lifetime commitment in repair mode.

Setting Boundaries

"We hold these truths to be self-evident, that all men are created equal, that they are endowed by their Creator, with certain unalienable Rights, that among these are Life, Liberty, and the pursuit of Happiness." You would know this is a famous quote from one of the most important US documents ever written: *The Declaration of Independence*. Particularly, it was a declaration that announced to Great Britain that the Thirteen Colonies: *New Hampshire, Massachusetts, Connecticut, Rhode Island, New York, New Jersey, Pennsylvania, Delaware, Maryland, Virginia, North Carolina, South Carolina, and Georgia* would regard themselves as thirteen independent sovereign states. Simply put, history would prove at the time, these were considered territories with internationally recognized boundaries under Britain's rulership.

Here is the caveat, these thirteen colonies wish to no longer be under British rule. History tells us that Britain began to tighten their control over the colonies, pass new laws that taxed the colonists, and even controlled their trade. How would you feel if foreign policies and decisions dictated your very life and well-being? The only way these thirteen colonies would cut ties or create boundaries from British rule would be to declare their independence: *finding their voice in the matter.*

Concerning marriage, this principle highlights the significance of defining a couple's voice. First, it instantly begins establishing what is affirmed in planning. Second, it works as a blueprint for the marriage. Again, in most cases, the voice of a marriage begins to develop when that man and woman make the initial effort to receive instructions in a pre-marital counseling setting. Third, the couple receives wisdom in counseling inspired by the Word of God. Finally, wisdom is used in times of difficulty that strengthen that voice for that marriage over time.

To the same degree, the Declaration of Independence gave thirteen colonies their voice to define who they were, both foreign and domestic; the voice developed within a marriage will also define it. Without this voice, any marriage can be easily *governed, influenced, and dictated by a foreign one.* In fact, during my research, I found out the word *foreign* in Greek; *Xeno* can give off two different connotations: negative or positive, contingent on context. *Xenos* can mean *stranger, enemy,* or even a *friend.* It stands the reason how once a familiar voice can become a stranger's voice when boundaries of that marriage are properly in place.

For instance, you might have once considered the advice of a family member or friend. However, when applying wisdom, their voice now seems less agreeable *to the terms* of your marriage. There appears to be a disconnect between what they are saying in comparison to what God is saying. John 10:5 (NKJV) tells us, "Yet they will by no means follow a stranger, but will flee from him, for they do not know the voice of strangers." As stated earlier in this book, a marriage is a spirit. Essentially, God has deposited a component of Himself within a marriage. It is this spirit that needs to be protected by that man and woman by placing *boundaries.* Creating boundaries around the marriage constitutes a willingness not to be influenced by anything *foreign.*

When Tanisha and I started, within our first year of marriage, creating boundaries was a topic she and I had to work on constantly. To be transparent, more so from my end. Mentally, I was still a single man, *learning how to become* a husband. Men, to be clear, I essentially had to cut off all other distractions or connections from female friends or associates from my past. "Does it take all of that?" Believe me; if there is an opening for a *voice of influence* to cause division in a home, it will seize the opportunity, make no doubt about it.

For me, boundaries consisted of intentionally removing these distractions and allowing my wife to have free access to my phone, passwords, and pins to every social media platform or any other account. As I stated before, anything you refuse to speak on, despite the reasons, will speak out for you later. One may think, "This sounds like a trust problem." Not at all. It demonstrates to my spouse that our marriage takes precedence over anything and anyone.

If you neglect to set boundaries, how can you possibly expect anyone else to respect the confines of your marriage? They are non-existent. This idea also applies to presenting your marriage accessible to anyone, or anything, at any time. In other words, there should be restrictions on who calls or text your spouse during certain times of the day. Now, please do not take this the wrong way. I am not insinuating you and your spouse to withdraw all communication from family, peers, and friends altogether and live on your own *created fantasy remote island*. However, I am implying that no one should have the privilege of withdrawing quality time from *family movie night* to discuss their entire day's sorrows—totally out of order and unacceptable. Boundaries inherently advocate balance, which will reverberate not only in the marriage but also throughout the home.

<u>"Like-Mind Connection" Wrap-Up:</u>

1. Have you and your spouse defined or considered boundaries within your marriage? How has placing these boundaries (defining your voice) helped you and your spouse in the area of prioritization?
2. What demands or expectations do you require of your spouse? Can they define them?
3. Do you now consider or have in times past considered your spouse as a "possession?"

Sex: Its Origin and Identity

"Christian teaching about sex is not a set of isolated prohibitions; it is an integral part of what the Bible has to say about living in such a way that our lives communicate the character of God."

~ROWAN WILLIAMS

It is almost taboo to associate the word *sex* with God without thinking in the context of a sinful act or perversion. Yet, as you can imagine, today, it is nearly impossible not to be exposed to sex in some manner. Whether through social media, an advertisement of an alcoholic beverage with women in bikinis on a beach, or maybe through the old infamous *cooler talk* often sparked up amongst people of common interest. The average individual is conveniently inundated with this subject so often that there appears to be a massive void between the two topics of discussion: *Sex and God, two worlds that seem light-years apart.* Seemingly, a distinct line of demarcation defines the two: *sin and holiness;* to violate this boundary is to violate an individual's chosen lifestyle.

As an adolescent, I recall participating in Sex Education from elementary school through middle school. These programs were considered life skills courses that enabled young people to make the right decisions when faced with challenging or uncomfortable scenarios related to either sex or puberty. The two topics were undoubtedly on nearly every young mind, however challenging to articulate in conversation. Learning the male and female reproductive system was thought of as a noble and innocent topic of discussion.

In reality, going through puberty for any adolescent could be pretty frustrating, embarrassing, and downright uneasy. However, through this avenue of learning, I can recall that this sparked more of an interest in the opposite sex as a young boy. The more I learned about my anomy, the more my curiosity expanded like a balloon. Honestly, it was as if I was attracted to nearly every girl that asked me to borrow a pencil or a sheet of paper while in class. Yup, I was in love. In my mind, they were all my girlfriends.

Nevertheless, as a teen and as a younger adult maturing in the kingdom faith, there were always underlining questions that needed to be answered: "Why do I have these urges, and I'm forbidden to fulfill them?" "Why can't I have sex with any woman of interest?" What's wrong with pornography?" Tragically, from experience and through observation, if left unaddressed or without any guidance, a person's reasoning will lead them into the "way that seems right to man, but its end is the way of death." – according to Proverbs 14:12 (NKJV). As a kingdom citizen and part of the church: the ecclesia; *the called-out ones*, we are mandated to answer these tough questions like: "How is sex associated with God?" I think we, the church, have erroneously separated sex from God to the extent it has created a massive void so many have fallen into involuntarily. For instance, if anyone tells a young person that sex outside of marriage is morally wrong but fails to identify where God is in sex puts them at a disadvantage in their understanding of the God Who created it.

This Thing Call Sex

Sex is first recorded in Genesis 4:1 (NKJV), as it tells us, "Now Adam knew Eve, his wife, and she conceived and bore Cain, and said, "I have acquired a man from the Lord." It is important to address here that the word "knew," translated in Greek, "ginosko" means to know intimately; *to learn to know*. Well, one might ask, "Why would Adam not have already *known* his wife if God made a woman from Adam's rib, an area which is close to the heart, the seat of the emotions? Should not that be indicative of closeness or intimacy?" Well, due to the couple's disobedience in the Garden of Eden, Adam now must become acquainted with the *fallen* or *sinful nature* of his wife, Eve. Thus, Eve's flesh now carries the weight of sin in which Adam instinctively grows to embrace, understand, and become sexually intimate.

Now there is a complex here that is too apparent to ignore. Out of the confines of which is holy; their marriage, the scripture tells us, "and she conceived, and bore Cain." The idea of *Cain* entering the world through the womb of Eve would be the precursor to *death* manifesting in the now fallen state of the world. Allow me to clarify. Romans 6:23 (NKJV) tells us that "For the wages of sin is death;" This constitutes not only physical death but a spiritual one. The plague of sin activated through one act of disobedience (Adam), transferred through the DNA of all humanity. Humanity is now in a constant fallen state in which he cannot control or manipulate within himself. Humankind is destined to die – Genesis 2:17 NKJV), "but of the tree of the knowledge of good and evil you shall not eat, for in the day that you eat of it you shall surely die."

Death must manifest itself to all humanity to the extent that it is not only apparent or perceptible but in concert leave behind a *sting*: a pain that reverberates for a length of time even after the injection of the poison. Thus, we see in Genesis 4:2 (NKJV), "Then she bore again, this time his brother Abel. Now Abel was a keeper of sheep, but Cain was a tiller of the ground." This scene sets the stage for sin's nature to manifest in man. Genesis 4:3—8 (NKJV) says, "And in the process of time it came to pass that Cain brought an offering of the fruit of the ground to the Lord. Abel also brought of the firstborn of his flock and of their fat. And the Lord respected Abel and his offering, but He did not respect Cain and his offering. And Cain was very angry, and his countenance fell. So, the Lord said to Cain, "Why are you angry? And why has your countenance fallen? If you do well, will you not be accepted? And if you do not do well, sin lies at the door. And its desire is for you, but you should rule over it." Now Cain talked with Abel, his brother, and it came to pass, when they were in the field, that Cain rose up against Abel his brother and killed him." Sin has now procreated itself.

Overall Purpose of Sex

Here is a popular question that I have heard before that should be addressed openly. "Does sex produce sin?" Not at all. The plague of sin was instituted into the fabric of man's DNA at the point of disobedience in Eden. However, sin now reigns in the mortal flesh of humanity in which we now wrestle with constantly. For Paul alludes to this in Romans 7:18 (NKJV), "For I know that in me (that is, in my flesh) nothing good dwells: for to will is present with me, but how to perform what is good I do not find." However, to address the question "Does sex produce sin?" one must first address the overall purpose of sex. If you can recall, in a previous chapter, I referenced Genesis 1:27—28 (NKJV), which says, "So God created man in His own image; in the image of God He created him; male and female He created them. Then God blessed them, and God said to them, "Be fruitful and multiply; fill the earth and subdue it; have dominion over the fish of the sea, over the birds of the air, and over every living thing that moves on the earth."

As a brief recap, under the umbrella of this command by God: *replicating His Spirit, which is His spiritual DNA, His fingerprint, throughout the earth is only one of two components to ensure this command is carried out. The other component is procreation: through sex.* Sex's primary intention was to *replicate little gods* in the Garden of Eden: subduing the earth. Once more, we learn in Genesis 2:7 (NKJV), God is now forming his *man* from the dust – (note that there is no sin in the earth), then breathed into his nostrils; and man became a living being.

Closeness, Transparency, and Intimacy

Later, God sees his man, Adam, alone. He then caused a sleep to fall over Adam and took a rib from him to form a woman. Through the vehicle of sex, the stage was set for Eden to be populated with little *gods*. It is also important here to note that in Genesis 2:25 (NKJV), scripture tells us, "And they were both naked, the man and his wife, and were not ashamed." Why? Before sin, both Adam and Eve walked in the apex of their spirituality; covering was unnecessary. Might I add, you only cover what you choose not to disclose. For the two of them had nothing to hide, instead everything to reveal. So it is in the Garden of Eden where *man* is naked and transparent before God. There were no barriers, only total embracement and communion with God the Father. Their nakedness in the Garden is symbolic of their *closeness, transparency, and intimacy* with God and with one another. For married couples, this should encourage us even more. It is not by coincidence that *closeness, transparency, and intimacy* are the three very attributes we see depicted from Jesus the Son, the Holy Spirit, and God the Father throughout scripture.

To reference closeness; John 5:19 (NKJV), "Then Jesus answered and said to them, "Most assuredly, I say to you, the Son can do nothing of Himself, but what He sees the Father do; for whatever He does, the Son also does in like manner." The closeness between a man and woman suggests there are parameters with which only the two have become familiar. Man and woman have identified their safe place of comfort and have created this space to share. As an addendum, without first establishing this space of closeness, the transparency and intimacy between that man and woman are incapable of developing and maturing. I would describe *closeness* as the catalyst or launching pad from which the latter evolves. Prayerfully, you will capture this in the following paragraphs.

Now to reference transparency between God the Father and the Son; Matthew 26:39 (NKJV), "He went a little farther and fell on His face, and prayed, saying, "O My Father, if it is possible, let this cup pass from Me; nevertheless, not as I will, but as You will." Transparency is simply a matter of the heart. In marriage, the husband and wife are now capable of sharing these mysteries and the deep-seated concerns they have toiled with, contemplated, or perhaps are afraid to disclose. As we see from the referenced scripture, the heart of Jesus was on display for God the Father to see His Son's humanity. He revealed his concerns, fears, contemplation, and even His *own will* right in that trying moment. That is to say; when there is a willingness for either spouse to become transparent, it reveals vulnerability. What this should then highlight between that man and woman is their dependency on one another. In other words*, should one become weak in an area, the other comes along aside to help strengthen their partnership.* Ultimately transparency presents the opportunity for ministry within the marriage—*it is the gateway to your help.*

Lastly, to reference intimacy, John 14:16 (NKJV) "And I will pray the Father, and He will give you another Helper, that He may abide with you forever." Amazing. Do you see that? Intimacy will blossom when there is transparency (the gateway for your help) between husband and wife. Thus, intimacy has found a place to *lay its head* in the marriage. Just as closeness is the grounds from which the other components of the relationship between God the Father, the Son, and the Holy Spirit are established, *intimacy secures it.* God the Father created within the design of sex, seclusively between man and woman, these very components of Himself: *closeness, transparency, and intimacy* to be experienced at the very nucleus of a marriage. Under the microscope for all humankind to see, we discover God Himself woven into the fabric of sex. In God's institution of marriage, He deposited within it *sex* to ensure and to affirm that what He has "joined together, let no man separate"— Matthew 19:6 (NKJV).

Profaning What is Holy

We can conclude that God created the very blueprint of sex in marriage for marriage. As we see, before Genesis Chapter 3, where the cunning serpent comes onto the scene, *sex as a creation of God* is set in its purest form. We will discover, the *closeness, transparency, and intimacy* between God and man would be sabotaged. Genesis 3:7—10 (NKJV), says "Then the eyes of both of them were opened, and they realized they were naked; so they sewed fig leaves together and made coverings for themselves. Then the man and his wife heard the sound of the Lord God as He was walking in the garden in the cool of the day, and they hid from the Lord God among the trees of the garden. But the Lord God called to the man, "Where are you?" So, he said, "I heard Your voice in the garden, and I was afraid because I was naked, and I hid myself."

Consequently, now that sin has infiltrated the earth and even man's heart, as it relates to sex, this same intensity of closeness, transparency, and intimacy conceived in the Garden acts as the very standard between man and woman in a marriage. God has intentionally placed the bar high. Nonetheless, for every married couple, you know that the idea of obtaining that place is always worthwhile in striving towards and protecting. In essence, God imputed within marriage sex as a memorial or as a reminder to indicate that only within the confines of marriage, *closeness, transparency, and intimacy* should always be imitated.

Due to the penalty of sin, the world has perverted this very act or idea of closeness, transparency, and intimacy of sex. To pervert is to essentially alter something from its original state and distort its overall purpose. For instance, man's perception is often perverted by their self-indulgence. What follows is an agreement between what they have envisioned and their desires. Jesus lays it out plainly for us in Matthew 5:28 (NKJV); "But I say to you that whoever looks at a woman to lust for her has already committed adultery with her in his heart."

Here is where deception is often conceived. We see this orchestrated with the woman Eve; right there in the garden in Genesis 3:6 (NKJV), "So when the woman saw that the tree was good for food, that it was pleasant to the eyes, and a tree desirable to make one wise, she took of its fruit and ate. She also gave to her husband with her, and he ate." We see the serpent methodically distort the image of a "tree of the knowledge of good and evil"; Genesis 2:17 (NKJV) into a "tree good for food" and a "tree desirable to make one wise."

Again, through the lenses of her appetite, what she imagines would be pleasurable to her, connected with her heart. In a moment, Eve now has a new belief system that has influenced her. What she has imagined, she now believes, will benefit her in the end. Notice what 2 Corinthians 10:5 (NKJV) says about these imaginations: "Casting down arguments and every high thing that exalts itself against the knowledge of God, bringing every thought into captivity to the obedience of Christ." The familiar phrase, *casting down* means to strike down. When you and I cast down these imaginations, we are striking down its *influence* the very moment it comes to thought. Without this discipline, these imaginations will begin to plant themselves in the very psyche of an individual, becoming their *new belief system*, a life they have been deceived into thinking they will ultimately benefit.

Simply put, a perverted picture projects a perverted life. Tragically, man has sought many vain and perverted ways to use sex to his sinful and selfish pleasures: *sex trafficking, pornography, rape, molestation, homosexuality, masturbation, orgies, and prostitution, to name a few.* Closeness, transparency, and intimacy can never be found in unclean, corrupt, and heinous activities. To think otherwise is to validate the work of deception presently in your life.

More than a Physical Act

The Bible defines sex outside of marriage as sexual immorality or simply: *fornication.* Have you ever wondered why the word "sex" rolls off the tongue much easier than the word "fornication" to the ordinary person? First, the obvious, the term "fornication" is not often used in today's dialogue amongst people. Secondly, but more importantly, to imply one *fornicates* or an individual as a *fornicator* addresses their sinful nature. Finally, it is to insinuate they need a Savior. A *sinner* does not know they are a sinner unless revealed to them by the unadulterated Word of God (Hebrews 4:12; NKJV).

To address fornication, the apostle Paul, in 1 Corinthians 6:13—20 (NKJV), enlightens the reader on the significance of this *physical and spiritual activity.* There are two critical takeaways from these scriptures concerning fornication:

1. *Anyone who fornicates becomes one in the flesh with their partner.* (1 Corinthians 6:16—17-NKJV)
2. *Anyone who fornicates sins against their own body.* (1 Corinthians 6:18 NKJV)

A few scriptures may reference these concepts; here is one of the few places where the idea of *soul ties* becomes paramount in the New Testament. But, it is also worth mentioning, the topic or actual phrase *soul ties*, like many other topics in the Bible, is often a controversial topic in that the exact phrase is never stated in the Bible at all. However, the term itself implies that two people are joined together in a life partnership: *as in a marriage*. For reference, Genesis 2:24 (NKJV)" Therefore a man shall leave his father and mother and be joined to his wife, and they shall become one flesh," and Mark 10: 8 (NKJV), "and the two shall become one flesh; so they are no longer two, but one flesh."

One thing to bear in mind is that we as human beings are a spirit, who possess a soul, encapsulated in a body: *mortal flesh*; which we will see referenced in Genesis 1:26 (NKJV), "And God said, Let Us make man in our image, after our likeness:" and in Genesis 2:7, "And the Lord God formed man of the dust of the ground, and breathed into his nostrils the breath of life; man became a living being." As you know, the body has five senses that assist it in surviving, experiencing, and enjoying the pleasures of this world. Good or bad, the experiences, memories, joys you and I have all enter into our souls (e.g., mind, will, and emotions) by way of these receptors of our flesh. They all help shape and mold how we view ourselves, the world, and others while here on earth. Ultimately, our souls make us unique, not just unique but also valuable to God and desirable to Satan. In essence, there is a war over our souls. Yes, *war*. 1 Peter 2:11 (NKJV) tells us, "Beloved, I beg you as sojourners and pilgrims, abstain from fleshly lusts which war against the soul;" A soul is lost without Jesus Christ in their life, which stresses the significance of Jesus the Christ being Savior of our very souls.

Rights Divided

When we *practice* fornication with multiple partners, we are *knitting our souls together* as one through intercourse. Again, 1 Corinthians 6:16—17 (NKJV) says, "Or do you not know that he who is joined to a harlot is one body with her? For "the two," He says, "shall become one flesh." But he who is joined to the Lord is one spirit with Him." Scripture then alludes to the fact that this is the only sin man sins against his own body. So we see here man is condemning himself and, by the act, agreeing to share all his *rights* to that of harlotry. Let that settle in. For example, I know people who could not fully invest themselves into a new and committed relationship due to their *divided rights* with someone they have known intimately prior. That is to say, as much as that sex partner occupied that individual's past, that sex partner in a spiritual context legally has much of a right being in their present and future. Here's why: Unless there is a renouncing of these soul ties, meaning an *abandonment or rejection* of these sexual partners, these rights from past partners, unfortunately, will continue to be exercised and a constant portrayal of that individual. This topic was one of the first intimate and transparent discussions I had with my wife before God. If the two of us were serious about moving forward together as life-long partners, renouncing these soul-ties (e.g., previous sexual partners, commitments, lovers, secrets, etc.) would have to be abolished and severed in the realm of the spirit. This discussion was not optional; it was mandatory.

Jesus insinuates this idea in a very familiar and controversial passage of scripture about the Samaritan woman in John 4:7—18 (NKJV); it reads: "A woman of Samaria came to draw water. Jesus said to her, "Give Me a drink." For His disciples had gone away into the city to buy food. Then the woman of Samaria said to Him, "How is it that You, being a Jew, ask a drink from me, a Samaritan woman?" For Jews have no dealings with Samaritans. Jesus answered and said to her, "If you know the gift of God, and Who it is Who says to you, "Give Me a drink," you would have asked Him, and He would have given you living water." The woman said to Him, "Sir, You have nothing to draw with, and the well is deep. Where then do You get that living water? Are You greater than our father Jacob, who gave us the well and drank from it himself, as well as his sons and his livestock? Jesus answered and said to her, "Whoever drinks of this water will thirst again, but whoever drinks of the water that I shall give him will never thirst. But the water that I shall give him will become in him a fountain of water springing up into everlasting life." The woman said to Him, "Sir, give me this water, that I may not thirst, nor come here to draw." Jesus said to her, "Go, call your husband, and come here." The woman answered and said, "I have no husband." Jesus said to her, "You have well said, "I have no husband," for you have had five husbands, and the one whom you now have is not your husband in that you spoke truly."

I Have No Husband

One key point I would like to highlight out of this scripture reference is this Samaritan woman's reply to Jesus was not that she was either a widow or even divorced. More specifically, in the Samaritan culture, women did not have the right to divorce their husbands, much as even wanting to come out in public about it. It was known primarily in the Bible days for women to be identified by their marital status. Should a woman not be married, the idea of a life of harlotry would be a category many women would risk falling into that day. Hence, Luke 7:36—39 (NKJV) "Then one of the Pharisees asked Him to eat with him. And He went to the Pharisee's house and sat down to eat. And behold, a woman in the city who was a sinner, when she knew that Jesus sat at the table in the Pharisee's house, brought an alabaster flask of fragrant oil, and stood at His feet behind Him weeping; and she began to wash His feet with her tears, and wiped them with the hair of her head, and she kissed His feet and anointed them with the fragrant oil. Now when the Pharisee who had invited Him saw this, he spoke to himself, saying, "This Man, if He were a prophet, would know who and what manner of woman this is who is touching Him, for she is a sinner."

Concerning this unnamed woman and Jesus, in this pivotal scene, Jesus brings a *buried secret* of this woman to the surface. Jesus tells her to go "call her husband." She tells Jesus, "I have no husband." In other words, she is telling Him, "I am not identified by any relational status (e.g., married, divorced, widow). She subliminally admits to Jesus that she lives a life that is unpleasing to the God of her ancestors. Jesus, in a rather casual way, responds to her: "You have well said, "I have no husband," for you have had five husbands, and the one whom you now have is not your husband in that you spoke truly."

Passage of scripture can be interpreted many different ways: "Did this woman have that many husbands and was divorced from all men?", "Would this be even possible in those days?", "What was Jesus alluding to when He made this comment?" I would suggest to you Jesus' comment lays it all out there right in the scripture. This anonymous woman has had several sexual relationships with anonymous partners who were husbands; husbands who were never her own. Jesus sees her soulish condition as being connected or having *soul-ties* with a total of 6 anonymous men (including the man she was with) who all were or are currently involved in adultery of their own. In love, Jesus presents her own life to her in a way only she could understand and grasp. For she says in John 4:19, (NKJV) "Sir I perceive that You are a prophet." Like many of us, this would be enough to drop our mouths and get our attention, a stranger who directly addresses our *skeletons in the closet*. Naturally, this would provoke us into opening our hearts to this Person and perhaps engage in a conversation, as we will see between this woman and Jesus.

Let's Talk It Out

In John 4:20-26 (NKJV), we then see this conversation between this Samaritan woman and Jesus almost immediately shifts into the topic of worship: *man's awareness of God's Holy Presence.* The woman begins to express to Jesus her ancestor's tradition in what they define as corporate worship. We can identify here that her perception of worship is erroneously connected to a physical location of the *past*. Ironically, much like her weary soul is still connected to her secret *past*. Her spirit (God-given) and soul are destitute and desire to connect to this *Living Water*.

She says to Jesus in John 4:20, "Our fathers worshipped on this mountain, and you Jews say that in Jerusalem is the place where one ought to worship." To attempt to give this text a 21st Century translation: *"Our people worshipped God here in this church for generations, while you Jews claim we must worship at another location."* Jesus replies to her, "You worship what you do not know; we know what we worship, for salvation is of the Jews. But the hour is coming and now is when the true worshipers will worship the Father in spirit and truth; for the Father is seeking such to worship Him."

Jesus implies to this woman that she and her people "draw near to God with their mouths, and honor God with their lips, but their hearts are far from God." – Matthew 15:8 (NKJV). This moment is ironic because she is unaware that the One she should worship is standing next to her. Knowing she is oblivious of Who He is, Jesus tells her in John 4:24 (NKJV), "God is spirit, and those who worship Him must worship in the Spirit and truth." That is, to truly worship the One and True Living God in Spirit and in Truth, salvation (this Living Water) must first be revealed. She responds in Matthew 4:25 (NKJV) by saying, "I know that Messiah is coming. When He comes, He will tell us all things,"; further addressing her spiritual condition, her thirst that has yet to be quenched. Jesus declares to her in Matthew 4:26 (NKJV), "I who speak to you am He." In a moment, I believe her eyes were open, her soul-ties immediately vanquish. Her life changed the very moment this Living Water was revealed and given to her.

In conclusion, the origin of sex is pure and unadulterated within the confines of marriage. Therefore, the overall intent of this chapter was to highlight sex's origin and identity primarily. This fact does not exempt addressing the good, the bad, and ugly of how humanity has defined sex. The identity and purpose of sex have received a negative connotation for centuries. Sin has projected an altered image to the world—an image *it* enjoys. It is without question God's institution of marriage should now become the forerunner in re-capturing and re-branding the embodiment of God's creation. To go a little further, the intent of an image, such as the *Golden Arches at McDonald's or the Swoosh logo at Nike,* is to express the idea or make-up of the product. Should a company decide to re-brand its product, its overall goal is to reach a wider audience or *reverse a bad reputation.* Hence, in my estimation, the institution of marriage should be more expressive in sharing the *image of sex* to a world seeking answers.

"Like-Mind Connection" Wrap-Up:

1. In what ways do you and your spouse intentionally protect the closeness, transparency, and intimacy within the confines of your bedroom?
2. Do you enjoy sexual intimacy with your spouse? Whatever your stance, begin to articulate that to your spouse.
3. What are you and your spouse's positions on soul-ties? Has addressing this topic presented clarity or closure in any aspect of the relationship?

Having a Proper Stance
in Understanding

"We are all unique. Don't judge;
understand instead."

~ Roy T. Bennett

For many married couples, disagreements at the beginning is an area many visit. One of the most tragic feelings for any person married is to live with their spouse in the same home without peace, without any solidarity. By default, this would provoke many couples to quit speaking to one another, permanently sleeping in different rooms, and ultimately driven to promiscuity.

As for my wife and I, we quickly realized that making what God is joining and building function and last would require constant communication from the two of us. We quickly realized this was an area that we could not afford to compromise under any circumstances. I like to think of communication as a designated posture one must learn to develop while in a marriage. Here is why: first, communication derives from the word *commune* or *communion,* in Greek is koinonia (koy-now-nee-uh), which means *fellowship* or *partnership*. Fundamentally speaking, this is what God has incorporated within marriage; this partnership or sharing of *the heart, ideas, plans, the future, fears, and even secrets.* Hence, communion.

Preparing Communion

To contextualize, during biblical times, it was accustomed in Jewish culture to sacrifice a Passover Lamb on the first day of the Festival of Unleavened Bread. In Mark 14:12 (NKJV), we see that the disciples asked Jesus, "Where do You want us to go and make preparations for you to eat the Passover?" Mark 14:13—16 (NKJV) tells us, "And He sent out two of His disciples and said to them, "Go into the city, and a man will meet you carrying a pitcher of water; follow him. Wherever he goes in, say to the master of the house, "The Teacher says, "Where is the guest room in which I may eat the Passover with My disciples?" Then he will show you a large upper room, furnished and prepared; there, make ready for us." So His disciples went out, and came into the city, and found it just as He had said to them, and they prepared the Passover."

Jesus, the Master Teacher, sitting with His disciples on what will be His last meal with all 12: *Peter, James (Son of Zebedee), John, Andrew, Bartholomew, James (the Lesser), Judas, Thaddeus, Matthew, Philip, Simon, and Thomas.* Instinctively, what may have begun in great joy and laughter, Jesus pivots and begins to communicate and share infectiously to all 12 disciples: *His heart, ideas, plans, the future, fears, and even secrets.* Jesus, in one moment, rows back the curtain of eternity for His followers to get a glimpse of what will come. Though the disciples were aware of the significance of the meal, they all, except for maybe one, were entirely unaware of this sacred moment with Jesus. The Bible lets us know that at the table are talks of *betrayal, the kingdom of God, this new covenant, blood, a broken body, and even death.* Yet, by the end of this great feast, *seeds of hope* were methodically planted in those men—except Judas. For 3 ½ years, Jesus invested into this small group who would then spread this Good News throughout the world.

Listening to the Heart

Regarding our communication or posture, this can simply be defined as positioning our bodies to begin listening. To not only the words coming out of an individual's mouth but also, more importantly, the heart of the person speaking as we would see in John's account in John 13:20—23 (NKJV). We see a certain disciple, as some theologians believe, possibly John, the youngest of the disciples, depict this exact posture. The passage reads, "Most assuredly, I say to you, he who receives whomever I send receives Me; and he who receives Me receives Him who sent Me. When Jesus had said these things, He was troubled in spirit and testified and said, "Most assuredly, I say to you, one of you will betray Me." Then the disciples looked at one another, perplexed about whom He spoke. Now there was leaning on Jesus' bosom one of His disciples, whom Jesus loved."

What is imperative to note here, John's position illustrated just where he was spiritually in his disposition to Jesus: *closest to His heart.* Here is where in my estimation, Jesus and John communicated on a more profound and spiritual level than the others. It was within his posture which permitted this young disciple not only to hear but perceive what Jesus was articulating at that table on that fateful night—which stands the reason why John, out of all the 12 disciples, was not martyred and given revelation on the things to come: *The Book of Revelations.* Not only is this encouraging but also a blueprint for any marriage to follow since within this same posture, where there is fellowship and partnership, we are then capable of communicating effectively to our spouses: *our heart, ideas, plans, the future, fears, and even secrets.*

Maintaining Good Posture

Anything that works well, you want to ensure that it continues its level of optimum performance. Whether an automobile, an electronic device such as a tablet, pc, cell phone, or even our bodies, we desire it to perform at its highest potential. There is a process with most electronic devices where the operating system undergoes what is usually known as system patching or, for context, maintenance. In short, this process allows the device to implement *internal processes* that will enable the operating system of that appliance to run more proficiently. As with an automobile, regularly scheduled maintenance such as oil changes, tire rotations, wheel alignments, spark plugs replacements would ensure the vehicle runs like the day you first drove it off the lot. Similarly, concerning our bodies, many may diet, exercise, or simply go on a much-needed vacation that would allow their body's vitals to recalibrate and perform at its highest level.

So, what am I saying? Anything deemed as having value or great worth requires maintenance; this includes our communication with our spouses. Yes, that is right; the popular "C-word": *communication.* As we have discovered earlier, John's posture was a position he not only desired to have with Jesus, but we see that by recognizing *great value,* he was capable of maintaining his posture for a significant length of time. Even after Jesus' accession into heaven. In like manner, the communication between you and your spouse must hold its posture through regularly scheduled maintenance: *identifying weaknesses and applying the necessary tools to strengthen its foundation.*

Notice I mentioned *scheduled* maintenance. The idea of scheduling is to make time or the effort to allow a window of time for an event. It says to the person or party that they are a priority and will be treated as such. For example, I can recall a few years into our marriage, Tanisha and I decided to go on an all-Inclusive *3-Day Marriage Retreat*, where we were gracious enough to have met with other like-minded married couples. Not only was the hotel beautiful, but our room was catered to us specifically. Itinerary, an impressive-welcomed letter, a bottle of wine, bed, and floor lightly decorated with soft rose petals, and romantic assignments we were to complete by the end of the day. The look my wife and I gave each other said it all: "We were in for a ride!"

Each day, the hosts, a married couple, focused on critical areas, such as communication, essential to a marriage. We performed great and meaningful exercises that were pertinent to the overall health of a sustaining marriage. This retreat allowed us as husband and wife to *revitalize, refocus, readjust, restructure*, and in some areas, *recommit* our first works over again.

In essence, we were undergoing our maintenance to sustain good posture in our marriage: *placing our ears over the hearts of one another and listening.* But for us to have undergone this maintenance, time was intentionally scheduled out of the busy rat race we were accustomed to daily. Since we both recognized the value in our communication, it was then critical to prioritize our communication: *regain* good posture for the much-anticipated journey ahead.

Laughter as the Connection

Where you will find laughter regularly carried out in a marriage, you will often find strong communication. Why? Naturally, laughter is a connection within itself, simply due to its contagious trait. It is nearly impossible not to crack a smile or experience a gut-wrenching laugh when you notice someone else laugh, see something amusing, or hear something hilarious as in a joke. It is due to this contagious trait that creates a social or interpersonal connection amongst people. Researchers have discovered that when a person laughs, a protein known as opioid receptors releases a chemical known as endorphins within the brain. As you might imagine, this chemical permits us to enter a euphoric place that makes us feel good for a moment. Now, considering the time restraints of this well-known sensation, the desire to often revisit this experience becomes addictive. When you laugh with your spouse, you instinctively yearn for another dosage.

Laughter within a marriage, in my estimation, only enhances communication, provokes interest in areas of concern, and nourishes the soul of both husband and wife alike. Tanisha and I have tested this principle so many times. This principle permitted us space to allow our sense of humor to thrive within our marriage. This space of laughter grants us the opportunity to use it at our disposal. For us, we often use it as our "little-handy-dandy" lifesaver we throw to one another when the waters seem a bit too high. There are times and seasons when a good laugh is needed: *loss of a close family member, an unexpected lay-off, a bad day on the job, a sick child, or when there could be tension in the house.* Laughter can communicate immediate healing, diffuse the tightest tension even in the direst of times. Proverbs 17:22 (NKJV) puts it this way: "A merry heart does good, like medicine, but a broken spirit dries the bones."

So, of course, every person has the choice to either get well emotionally by taking the *medicine of laughter* or choosing to stay in a brittle place expecting to get better. As for my house, the *lifesavers* we have often thrown to one another enabled us to be reeled back to a place of safety, ensuring that our communication with one another stays *afloat*. In the words of the late great comedy legend Charlie Chaplin: "To truly laugh, you must be able to take your pain and play with it!"

Breach the Trust, Sabotage the Communication

I am beyond grateful for my secular career as a cybersecurity analyst. This field has enabled me to connect with the brilliant minds of people from various backgrounds and skillsets. Moreover, by God's grace, this path has afforded me the luxury to learn from great leaders, attend world-renowned Cyber Security seminars, and continue to grasp an understanding of the many technologies and challenges the field faces almost daily.

In brief, cybersecurity is the process of protecting a company's or organization's *Confidentiality*: the state of keeping private, *Integrity*: ensuring information is not maliciously modified, and *Availability*: keeping accessibility to data or service; well-known as the CIA Triad. When any of these three triad components are compromised undetected, the reliability of the defense-in-depth approach or barriers methodically put in place to protect an organization is no longer trusted or questioned. Primarily, the term often used is *breached*, breaking through a barrier, or causing a gap. There is a *level of trust* that has been violated or degraded. The infrastructure (e.g., firewall, anti-malware software, Multi-factor authentication) that once communicated *trust* now communicates *uncertainty*. There is now a false sense of security shared within the organization. In other words, the message that was once being communicated is now sabotaged. You would then imagine; this is not the most comfortable place for any security analyst to be.

Similarly, within God's institution of marriage, where there is often a breach of trust between spouses, there is always sabotage of communication without fail. Moreover, when there is a breach (gap) of communication, there is often sabotage of trust—trust and communication work simultaneously. They complement each other. It is impossible to have one without the other.

Our adversary, Satan, is quite aware of this simple principle and will work it double-time against the husband and wife, often undetected, to his advantage to breach the validity of trust between spouses. Understand that his methodology or entryway is contingent on what is *most* vulnerable. This principle can be observed throughout history. Satan instinctively exploits this principle to his advantage to not only strengthen his kingdom on earth but to go as far as establishing it within a marriage. The deceiver is incapable of creating anything new. He only has a specific set of devices (2 Corinthians 2:11-NKJV) accessible to him. He meticulously uses this tactic on God's people, and this simple principle is towards the top of the list.

The Principle at Work

To help illustrate this point, a prevalent biblical character, Saul, Israel's first King, experienced this principle working against him firsthand. Nonetheless, it is imperative to stress that Saul was only elected king due to Israel desiring a king like all the surrounding nations. A king that would lead them, a king that would go before them, fight their battles, *clear the path*, and be their appointed hero. To put it plainly, he was the *people's choice, the people's elect*. Now, did God initially disapprove of the young man Saul? Not at all. He was only displeased with Israel's rejection of Him as their One and only King. 1 Samuel 8:6—7; (NKJV) "But the thing displeased Samuel when they said, "Give us a king to judge us." So Samuel prayed to the Lord. And the Lord said to Samuel, "Heed the voice of the people in all that they say to you; for they have not rejected you, but they have rejected Me, that I should not reign over them."

To be placed in this excellent and prominent position as the new king of God's people, there was only one prerequisite for this young king, *the people's elect*, which was *to listen to the Word of the Lord*. Sounds easy enough, right? However, listening requires hearing what is said to understand, then following through; this is known as *active listening*.

On the same day, Saul is anointed king over Israel; scripture allows readers to witness God, through Samuel give Saul his first significant set of instructions in 1 Samuel 15:1—3 (NKJV), "Samuel also said to Saul, "The Lord sent me to anoint you king over His people, over Israel. Now, therefore, heed the voice of the words of the Lord. Thus says the Lord of hosts:" I will punish Amalek for what he did to Israel, how he ambushed him on the way when he came up from Egypt. Now go attack Amalek, and utterly destroy all that they have, and do not spare them. But kill both man and woman, infant and nursing child, ox and sheep, camel and donkey."

By the time we get to verses 8—9 of the same chapter, Saul does the complete opposite from what He was instructed to do from the Lord. Scripture says, "And he took Agag the king of the Amalekites alive, and utterly destroyed all the people with the edge of the sword. But Saul and the people spared Agag, and the best of the sheep, and of the oxen, and of the fatlings, and the lambs, and all that was good, and would not utterly destroy them: but everything that was vile and refuse, that they destroyed utterly." Notice where the Word of Lord returned to, God's mouthpiece: *Samuel*, indicative of disobedience or rejection of the Word of the Lord. 1 Samuel 15:10—11 (NKJV), "Now the Word of the Lord came to Samuel, saying, "I greatly regret that I have set up Saul as king, for he has turned back from following Me, and has not performed My commandments. And it grieved Samuel, and he cried out to the Lord all night." Here we see when there is a gap or breach in communication, trust is then sabotaged. God cannot trust the people's elect; therefore, God rejected Saul as their king.

No Trace of Breach

Strangely, suppose we were to trace back and do a complete *analysis* on these recent events. In that case, there is no indication of Satan himself in scripture from the time God, through Samuel, gives

Saul these instructions in 1 Samuel 15:3 (NKJV) to the moment Saul disobeys in 1 Samuel 15:8—9 (NKJV). Like any well-carried out breach, as expected, Satan's influence of disobedience or rebellion goes completely undetected. Saul mysteriously goes from hearing and disobeying the Word of the Lord in a matter of a couple of verses. As onlookers, we only witness the aftermath of this breach.

It appears Saul, within a small window of time, seems to be under the influence of rebellion which permitted him to disobey God's command completely, without any regard. Thus, the only *evidence* we find in scripture that points to Satan is the disobedience or rebellion of Saul, an unwillingness to follow God. For context, this is a prominent trait of Lucifer, as we discovered in 1 Samuel 15:11(NKJV), "for he has turned back from following Me, and has not performed My commandments."

The way an ordained marriage of God disarms the principles of darkness from disrupting their communication is by choosing to live by the principles of God, which is His Word. Your security is only as good as your greatest defense mechanism. When moral principles are in place and practiced, a false sense of security would less likely be the outcome.

"Like-Mind Connection" Wrap-Up:

1. Is the communication between you and your spouse laborious or effectual? Explain why. What are areas you can improve?
2. When was the last time your marriage had a *spiritual tune-up*? Are there any events scheduled for the two of you to invest back into the relationship? If not, plan a lovely retreat.
3. Can you laugh with your spouse? In what ways has laughter enriched the overall marriage? Do you see laughter as a tool?

Skill of Balancing

*"Balance is a feeling derived from being whole
and complete; it's a sense of harmony. It is essential
to maintaining quality in life and work."*

~ JOSHUA OSENGA

Married life is a life of constant balancing. Another word for *balance* I would prefer is *well-managed*, the ability to readjust and reallocate your time due to the often demands and the uncontrollable dynamics of a typical day. While on earth, time is an asset you and I have acquired from God to manage. How well you and I manage this asset dictates our productivity on this side of eternity. Time management is by in large a skill. Like any other skill, it requires *discipline, desire, focus, and patience* over a length of time to see the expected results begin to manifest.

Nonetheless, in my opinion, time management is not at all a skill in which another person teaches you; instead, it is a skill that is first developed by simply observing the principle by which the person or object lives daily. Then follows the discipline, desire, focus, and patience mentioned previously. Finally, observing constitutes watching a person or thing intently to acquire the principle to gain leverage in the area of deficiency.

My days as a single younger man, my lifestyle reflected just how well I managed my time, make no mistake about it. Try imagining one of the largest well-known city's busiest intersections without traffic lights. See the picture? For instance, during my most-earliest years in undergrad, time management was not even a skill I deemed a necessity. Unfortunately, what I often witnessed around me impulsively became the tradeoff; the heavy drinking, excessive partying, the women, skipping classes were all my norm. It is safe to say; I was simply a follower. Wherever the crowd was, I made it my plan to be somewhere in the midst. I learned this was the principle I chose to observe; this was the principle I decided to follow; this was the principle I mainly identified in myself. It will be by this same principle in which I will reap a life headed on the decline.

Lesson of Observation

After the many personal dead-ends, failures, mistakes, and grief I experienced along this downward spiral, only by the grace of God, in turn, I gave my life to Christ Jesus. Soon after, I became a part of a local church assembly, served God's people, and plugged into the heart of the man of God, my pastor to this day; Dr. Thomas A. DeLoach of Word of Life Outreach Ministries. Though I have given my life to Jesus during this time, time management was still a skill I had not yet possessed, as my personal life needed to be balanced, disciplined, and tuned to the many demands of my life during that time.

Over the many years of faithfully serving at this church, I observed just how my spiritual father was able to adjust and schedule his life. As much as I learned from what he said from the pulpit, I realized I learned as much or even more from just observing his life. To be clear, it was not the man I studied as much as it was the principle in which he lived by that structured his life that I embraced. In brief, observation permits an individual to learn while yet on the move. I had the heart to continue moving in the right direction. Through practice, I decided to apply the discipline, desire, focus, and patience to the principle I observed at work.

Go to the Ant

To further drive this philosophy, the richest king of Israel, King Solomon, is considered the wisest man who has ever lived. In 1 Kings 3: 5—15 (NKJV), God appears to young Solomon in a dream and initiates dialogue. He says to Solomon, "Ask! What shall I give you?" Solomon then replies to God, "You have shown great mercy to your servant, David, my father, because he walked before You in truth, in righteousness, and in uprightness of heart with You. He continues by saying, "Now, O LORD my God, You have made Your servant king instead of my father David, but I am a little child; I do not know how to go out or come in. And Your servant is in the midst of Your people whom You have chosen, a great people, too numerous to be numbered or counted. Therefore, give to Your servant an understanding heart to judge Your people, that I may discern between good and evil. For who is able to judge this great people of Yours?" We then learned that this response pleased the Lord, and God not only gave him a "wise and discerning heart," but He also gave this young king both "riches and honor."

We see here, now a young king, given a massive task of ruling and governing a kingdom he has inherited from his father, King David. Indeed, there would be the constant demands from people, scheduled meetings with his counsel, and choices he as king would have to make, influencing Israel as a nation. How would he then make his time work for him instead of against him? Fortunately,

King Solomon, famously known for writing the book of Proverbs, could observe the principles amid his world through wisdom. Embedded within nature expressed core principles Solomon would possess as his very own. Let us look at Proverbs 6:6—11 (NKJV); it says, "Go to the ant, you sluggard!" Consider her ways and be wise, which having no captain, overseer, or ruler, provides her supplies in the summer and gathers her food in the harvest. How long will you slumber, O sluggard? When will you rise from your sleep? A little sleep, a little slumber, a little folding of the hands to sleep. So shall your poverty come on you like a prowler and your need like an armed man."

Doing the Unthinkable

Solomon calls this person represented in this passage as a sluggard, a term that references a slothful individual in his planning. Time is not as valuable to this person, much less their own life. "Hmm, I think I may know this person." The scripture then tells this person who is void of understanding to consider or observe a more excellent way of living. Yes, to do the *unthinkable*. You often understand or grasp a new way of thinking by first observing, generally, not in the noise, but the stillness; not in the grand, but the small details of life.

I can recall in Luke 15:17 (NKJV) the story of the prodigal son; when he was faced with hunger, contemplated eating from the pods from which the swine fed, to considering his father's hired servants who had more than enough bread to go around. What clicked? What changed? Here is the clue: This young man was able to come to himself by simply observing his consideration of a life of abundance versus a life of scarcity. Right there, in his *stillness*, while taking in the harsh stench and a more *detailed* look of the organic matter from each pod, introduced him to this new reality. There is a principle of abundance in which he now observes operating within his father's house while at the same time observing the principle of scarcity working right in the mud he now finds himself wallowing in. This revelation helped this young man make the *best* decision.

Often the principles you choose to see are the principles you take up. The good news is that *options* are always available to you and me. During undergrad, the principles I chose only to see were the principles I was governed by at the time. Referring back to Proverbs 6:6—11 (NKJV), Solomon urges to pay attention to the *small details*, the ant; how she conducts business without any superiority to instruct her; yet knows when to "provide her supplies in the summer" and "gather her food in the harvest." The ant instinctively knows that the quality of her life depends on just how well she manages her greatest asset: *her time*. She fully understands the principle of time management. Whether through a person or discovered in nature, the ability to first observe this principle of allocating your time increases your productivity.

Schedule Your D.A.Y.

If you could be completely transparent, you once have stated it or even thought of it: "There is just not enough time in a day." Busyness has a peculiar way of elapsing time. I like to portray *busyness* as a modern-day time capsule within itself. Once you are strapped in, time appears to only leave behind traces of the past. Busyness can be defined as simply going from one task to the next without any real, meaningful correlation. What usually drives us is this simple logic: "It has to get done." In my estimation, we are all guilty of this. For any married couple, especially with children, or simply anyone for that matter, who is confronted with the constant dynamics of a typical day, you can most certainly identify with this statement.

I have discovered a principle when having the "It has to get done" mentality. As it concerned my marriage, in the beginning, I found that the more I accomplished, the more puffed up I became, or in some cases, even downright arrogant due to my accomplishments. Mentally it became a game to me in which I compared the number of duties I accomplished around the house within a day to the number of responsibilities my wife did.

Talk about *keeping score*. To some degree, the outcome of knowing I outworked my wife stroked my ego in some peculiar way—this permitted me to complain or even have ill-will towards her if she was in the deficit. Irrational thoughts seem to stay idle in my mind. Yes, I admit; very immature and unfair.

I have observed this is a very familiar principle that many have witnessed in others or personally within themselves. It is even found in scripture concerning two close sisters: Mary and Martha in Luke 10:38—42 (NKJV). The text reads: "Now it happened as they went that He entered a certain village, and a certain woman named Martha welcomed Him into her house. And she had a sister called Mary, who also sat at Jesus' feet and heard His word. But Martha was distracted with much serving, and she approached Him and said, "Lord, do You not care that my sister has left me to serve alone? Therefore, tell her to help me." And Jesus answered and said to her, "Martha, Martha, you are worried and troubled about many things. But one thing is needed, and Mary has chosen that good part, which will not be taken away from her.

A D.A.Y. in God

Two sisters, two people, two agendas; both having "sat at Jesus' feet and heard His Word." They were both fully aware of Who He was—God in the flesh, Jesus the Christ. So here is the dilemma: Martha decides to schedule her day *for her God*, while Mary schedules her *day in God*. As someone who loves to serve the needs of people, I can personally empathize with Martha because her heart was indeed in the right place. I think we all can agree with that. However, Martha has a servant's heart, a desire to serve the Master.

Regrettably, her "It has to get done" mentality has cost her the ability to recognize a significant moment she will never experience. Jesus replies to Martha and says, "Martha, Martha, you are worried and troubled about many things. But one thing is needed, and Mary has chosen that good part, which will not be taken away from her." Right in this particular moment, Martha's spiritual disposition is looking from the outside. Her disposition has placed her at a disadvantage in partaking in the good part. Here is why: Acts 17:28 (NKJV) reminds us, "For in Him we live, and move, and have our being." Mary must have received the memo and followed through; she was determined to schedule her day *in* God.

D.A.Y. is an acronym for *Decisions, Attitude, and Yourself.* How we live, move, and have our being in God speak to how we acclimate our *decision-making, attitude in critical moments, and even a self-evaluation of our mental, physical, and spiritual health.* My friend, this is significant in our day-to-day life as a follower of Jesus. Any D.A.Y. scheduled outside of God often comes with tiredness, anxiety, pressures, and feeling overwhelmed. As we witnessed, Martha became acquainted with in Luke 10:40 (NKJV); "But Martha was distracted with much serving, and she approached Him and said, "Lord, do You not care that my sister has left me to serve alone? Therefore, tell her to help me."

Jesus' response to Martha's *S.O.S call* was not in the manner in which Martha may have had in mind; instead, more importantly, it was in a way she could quickly grasp and articulate; "you are worried and troubled about many things." Ouch. Simply put, "Martha, your D.A.Y. is simply *out of sync* and needs realignment." I cannot count how many times I have had this same *realignment* problem. Multiple bumps in the road, or what I would describe as *temporary stressors,* would consequently misalign my focus, and I find myself annoyed or frantic. Friend, I can assure you, this is not the most comfortable place to be.

On the contrary, Mary, her sister, scheduled her D.A.Y. *in* such a way that afforded her not to miss out on this crucial moment with Jesus. She was in the right place at the right time, which permitted her to enter a place of true worship, tuning into the heart of Jesus right there again, at His feet. In my estimation, this is unquestionably the very place where any faithful follower of Jesus Christ desires to be. There at His feet, Mary finds *balance.*

Embrace the Place

As much as Jesus was the Son of God, He also was man enough that He needed to exercise this same principle to ensure He stayed well-balanced and followed God's will. The Gospels: *Matthew, Mark, Luke, and John* all give an account of how Jesus would intentionally set aside a time; often in the early mornings or late evenings in His *D.A.Y.* by going off in a lonely and remote place to pray and be with the Father: Mark 1:35 (NKJV), "Now in the morning, having risen a long while before daylight, He went out and departed to a solitary place; and there He prayed."; Luke 6:12 (NKJV), "Now it came to pass in those days that He went out to the mountain to pray, and continued all night in prayer to God."

It is important to clarify here that this was not only His routine; instead, this was His source of actually seeing what was indeed on the heart of God; His Father. From reading the scriptures, we see this was His lifestyle. Is this not the desire for every faithful follower of Jesus? To know the nature of God, to understand the Father's deepest desires? John 5:19 (NKJV) illustrates this perfectly; it says: "Then Jesus answered and said to them, "Most assuredly, I say to you, the Son can do nothing of Himself, but what He sees the Father do; for whatever He does, the Son also does in like manner." This statement echoes the actual dependency of the Father. Yet, this would, in fact, not be possible had Jesus not decided to leave behind both the jeers and cheers of the crowd and even his own emotions; to embrace a place with God to receive divine instructions.

We later observe that His time was neither wasted nor lost through His disposition with the Father, instead delegated effectively. In every way, both Father and Son were in synch—this could justify John 21:25 (NKJV); "And there are also many other things that Jesus did, which if they were written one by one, I suppose that even the world itself could not contain the books that would be written. Amen." Wow, talking about walking in purpose. Jesus' D.A.Y., in much the same way as Mary's D.A.Y., was tuned in such a way that His *decision-making, attitude in critical moments, self-evaluation of his mental, physical, and spiritual health* was persuaded by being centered in God the Father. At heart, salvation for all of humanity hinged upon Jesus' D.A.Y.

To help drive my point, from the time Jesus is led by the Spirit into the wilderness to be tempted by the devil to the cross on the hill of Golgotha, we see Jesus' D.A.Y. tested in ways unimaginable. First, his decision-making: Matthew 4:1—4, (NKJV) "Then Jesus was led by the Spirit into the wilderness to be tempted by the devil. After fasting forty days and forty nights, he was hungry. The tempter came to him and said, "If you are the Son of God, tell these stones to become bread." Jesus answered, "It is written: "Man shall not live on bread alone, but on every word that comes from the mouth of God." Secondly, His attitude in critical moments: Luke 22: 42— 44 (NKJV) – "Father, if it is Your will, take this cup away from Me; nevertheless, not My will, but Yours, be done." Then an angel appeared to Him from heaven, strengthening Him. And being in agony, He prayed more earnestly. Then His sweat became like great drops of blood falling down to the ground."

Lastly, highlighting his overall health; spirit, body, and mental state: John 19:28—30, (NKJV), "After this, Jesus, knowing that all things were accomplished, that the Scripture might be fulfilled, said, "I thirst!" Now a vessel full of sour wine was sitting there, and they filled a sponge with sour wine, put it on hyssop, and put it to

His mouth. So, when Jesus had received the sour wine, He said, "It is finished!" And bowing His head, He gave up His spirit." We can conclude then, Jesus' worst D.A.Y. of significant testing inherently gave humanity new life, our D.A.Y. of salvation. What you and I would naturally describe as a bad D.A.Y., Jesus had every right to become selfish and hold onto His life; yet He still chose us. What god is like our God? 2 Corinthians 6:2 (NKJV) says, "For He says: "In an acceptable time I have heard you, and in the day of salvation I have helped you. Behold, now is the accepted time; behold, now is the day of salvation."

How is your D.A.Y. aligned to ensure life resonates with those connected to you as a single or spouse? How does this affect you? Where is your D.A.Y.'s disposition as it relates to the center of God's heart? Is God your True Source? In my estimation, these are tough questions. Still, essential questions one must ask themselves to begin to take inventory of their decision-making, attitude, and overall health as a follower of Jesus. According to John 15:5 (NKJV), if God is indeed the Vine, and His children are the branches, I must then believe there is a *place of balance* and *sufficiency* for me in my D.A.Y. in God.

"Like-Mind Connection" Wrap-Up:

1. Time management is a skill that assists in evaluating priorities within a given day. Is this a skill in which both or one spouse needs to approve?

2. How do you plan your "D.A.Y.?" Is there a regiment you follow daily? How has this helped you in your marriage or family?

3. Is your "D.A.Y." out of sync? What adjustments can you and your spouse make together to recalibrate the marriage's overall decisions, attitude, and health?

Two Hearts, One Mind, One God

*"Physical maturity is bound to time. Spiritual
maturity is bound to obedience."*

~ JOHN BEVERE

A s we draw to the last chapter of this book, it is my deepest
prayer that you, the reader, have a better perspective and
greater appreciation of the sacred union of marriage and of the
One Who created it. As God is towards the children of God, the
wedding ring exchanged between husband and wife symbolizes a
circle, an infinite, never-ending *love commitment*. God is this total
embodiment and standard of Love. To contextualize, Jesus is the
Symbol of God's Love commitment for all of humanity; for John
3:16 (NKJV) tells us, "For God so loved the world, that He gave His
only begotten Son, that whoever believes in Him should not perish
but have everlasting life." Thus, Jesus was committed unto death
for all of humanity.

Unlike Jesus, often where there is a professing of a commitment
by an individual, either time or resistance appears to extinguish
excitement, motivation, and even desire. But, ultimately, this

confirms and reveals the genuineness of the person's heart on day one. As the old saying goes, "Time reveals all things."

As an illustration, you tell yourself you are going to remodel your bathroom. You have imagined the colors, the theme, and all the intricate details of the project. Without any proper investment, days become weeks, weeks turn into months, months turn into years, years turn into *never.* Though the bathroom is still functional, there is no longer a motivation nor desire to follow through on the professed commitment. The brand new *HGTV inspired* bathroom renovation remains just an idea that never lifted off the ground— this reveals the true heart of the individual from day one; they were never *entirely* on board with their commitment. You should never view your marriage as an *HGTV project*; instead, a promise you vowed to your spouse in the sight of God.

Two Hearts

At this time, I would like to end where I began. Much like the wedding ring, again symbolizing a circle, an infinite never-ending love commitment, to expound on the significance of this book's theme: *Two Hearts, One Mind, One God.* This theme reverberates a gradual and steady progression of both the man and woman to see God displayed strongly in their marriage, which in turn requires a great commitment to one another. Yes, as it pertains to my wife and me, our *two hearts* somehow found one another through a very unorthodox way, yet it would be our thinking that has kept us together through the years. To give a backdrop of our story, I would like to share my wife's portrayal of events leading up to our meeting as she remembered, for she is just more detailed. I mean, she can recall the temperature and the humidity a year ago from today; she is that spot on. First, however, to gain insight on *Two Hearts, One*

Mind, One God theme, I would like to share her perspective on how it all began: illustrating *Two Hearts* coming together:

"I knew that my single days were coming to an end. I began having conversations with my best friends about my future husband, when we would get married, and where we would live. The only problem was, I had no prospects. I was single, single. I joined a dating website, and after several failed attempts at meeting the man of my dreams, I deleted all my accounts. What was another year of being single anyway? I still had an earnest desire to meet my spouse, and I had high expectations of him. Ladies, you know the list that we humbly create with modest expectations of the man who does not have to be perfect. Reading through my list of physical features, I began to question if my future husband had the exact irrelevant requirements.

So, I began to work on myself. I started going to the dentist for teeth whitening, treating myself to facials, exercising regularly, and going to the hair salon more frequently. Although I was spending a lot of money, my now husband will tell you that I invested in our marriage. However, I like to think of it as I was preparing naturally for what was happening in the spiritual. Although I could not articulate what the Holy Spirit was doing at the time, I now know that I was in my season of preparation. Please understand that I am not referring to my physical appearance and being attractive to my potential spouse. But it was something much more profound. I was preparing my heart and spirit to receive a gift that God had been waiting for me to unwrap.

God had me change my list from physical features to godly characteristics. My list began to sound more comprehensive than unrealistic, including things like "let him love God more than he loves himself." After all my online dating, impatiently waiting for the right man to approach me, I was convinced that my man had fallen off the face of the planet. So, imagine my surprise when my cousin decided to share my phone number with a stranger. I reluctantly took the call from this stranger, and we had a five-hour conversation.

I would love to say that this was the best conversation ever, and I knew that this guy was the one, but no, he just talked too much, and I could not get a word in so that I could hang up and go to bed. For some reason, we tried the next day again, and it was less torture once he learned my name. Our conversations became more tolerable and more insightful as we sang R&B songs over the phone. Finally, we decided that it was time to meet face to face since I would be in his town for two weeks. Up until this point, we had only seen two or three photos of one another. Upon meeting in person, we had the best time. We were similar in many ways, sharing laughter, enjoying the competition, and our all-time favorite: eating. The first two weeks of our meeting were amazing, like a breath of fresh air that I never knew existed. We enjoyed each other's company so much that I just knew he wanted to be my best friend and nothing else. I was staying with my cousin for those two weeks, and the last night I was in town, I told her that this guy was going to be my husband, even though he only wanted to be my friend. I was wrong, and he felt the same way I did. He would not let me leave town without agreeing to be exclusive."

Dating the Mask

Tanisha's account embodies how *Two Hearts*: again, signifying the humanity, physical attraction, imperfections, mistakes, and even man's willingness, engage in an all-exclusive relationship. While I was in my preparation stages of being the person to whom God would join me, if you can recall, there was also great preparation on her part. Not only in the physical but also in the spiritual. What I can appreciate from her was that she was intentionally putting herself in the ideal posture to be found according to Proverbs 18:22 (NKJV); "He who finds a wife finds a good thing and obtains favor from the Lord." Posture has everything to do with it. According to the Bible, you and I cannot worship unless we worship *in Spirit and in truth.*—this is not optional; it is a requirement.

Ironically, you would begin to believe that these would all be good indicators because of a couple's preparation, similarities, physical attractions, shared laughter, date nights, emotional enticement of the hearts, and even posture*s*. Thus, you would assume that they would be well equipped for a life-long commitment at first glance. But, as I once heard before, the first time you meet someone, you often meet their representative; never the real person, only the mask they have decided to pick up and wear. Mistakenly, here is where many people "drop the ball even before they pick it up." They consider marriage with the *person* they just met rather than with the *person* they truly are.

Now, of course, in marriage, there will always be something you are learning about your spouse. That is the beauty of it— this speaks to the overall progression of the union, the maturity of two harmonious individuals assisting one another to become better versions of themselves each day. But, on the contrary, I would like to clarify that Tanisha and I have witnessed many individuals learning and adapting to the *mask* of their significant other, yet never considering their true identity, which is why we stress the significance of the pre-marital counseling process.

Not only do the pre-marital counseling sessions assist in dialing into the person's intentions, but it shows an illustration of the spouses' morals and integrity by disclosing sensitive yet necessary answers to questions like: "Why do you want to marry?" "What are your plans for this marriage?" "Who are you accountable to?" "How would you define your relationship with Jesus?" "How do you view sex outside of marriage?" and "How do you handle disagreements?" Asking the right questions in a safe setting aids in lowering the *mask of the heart* little by little, inch by inch.

It is important to stress that if any man or woman claims to take their marriage seriously but is unwilling to consider pre-marital counseling, they deliberately never consider it *successful* from the start. Here is why—any militia veteran would agree that before they go into battle against the enemy, they would first consider and learn the best techniques, tactics, advice, or strategy from their military superiors. The sergeant or general then delegates the strategy to the militia needed to complete the mission's overall goal. Without the imperative planning of the militia, carelessly moving into unknown territory would risk many causalities. So yes, marriage to a young couple is an *unfamiliar territory* that needs special preparation and guidance before deployment. Proper planning and strategizing in pre-marital counseling communicates to their significant other that their life does matter, and the life the two will soon share will not count as another casualty.

One Mind

As we make the transition from *Two-hearts*, looking back, shockingly, the couple now sees that all the emotionalism they had experienced at the beginning that attracted them together will not necessarily keep them together. Seeing that marriage is a spiritual entity within itself, created by God, emotionalism is then vetted out to begin testing what is discovered in what is commonly referred to as the *honeymoon* stage. I want to stress again; marriage is a spirit, a union between man, woman, and God. So, while you and your spouse are instinctively drawing closer to experiencing God in the marriage, the very composition of the marriage institution is gradually becoming more evident.

To better put it, the philosophy of just *hooking up to see if it will work out* now enters an atmosphere or domain where everything of the natural struggles to coexist with what is spiritual. What is established on earth cannot thrive on its own at this altitude. Due to the resistance or inability to adapt and adjust in this *space*, most marriages suffocate by attempting to live from earthly principles.

They are not willing to work through difficulty with the mind of Christ. Now, I know that may not sound *deep* or *revelatory*, but when the rubber meets the road, how the two together overcome the most strenuous and challenging times are contingent on how the two think as one, hence *like-minds*.

To attempt to put Jesus' mind under a microscope per se, let us see how He thinks about every problem known to man. John 16:33 (NKJV) says, "These things I have spoken to you, that in Me you may have peace. In the world, you will have tribulation, but be of good cheer, I have overcome the world." In marriage, both persons must know Jesus has overcome the world—this should not be a superficial or fabricated way of thinking. Rather a truth, both have agreed to move forward with to tackle every circumstance they may face, whether it be: *financial, unforgiveness, hurt, loss, sickness, betrayal, parenting, substance abuse, and even death.*

Agree, Lift, Stabilize, and Move

As I mentioned earlier in this writing, having the mind of Christ is the kind of attitude you need in adversity, especially when working within a partnership. You cannot expect to see your marriage move forward from day to day, thinking differently, namely having two different opinions on a strategy or management of shared responsibilities under one roof. For instance, if two people need to pick up a heavy piece of furniture to move it across a room yet have two different methodologies without ever agreeing, the task will be more than likely unsuccessful. However, thinking *like-minded* permits the task to be a success and less strenuous on the two. This analogy reflects challenges becoming minimized when both husband and wife can first: *Agree, Lift, Stabilize and Move* together in one direction.

Double-mindedness can be defined as paralysis of the mind—it counteracts principles with another set of principles. For instance, if we were to take this same couple and halfway through the move, the two decide to be influenced by another set of principles contrary to the one already in place, there will certainly be a different outcome. Instead of *Agreeing,* the couple would *Disagree.* Instead of *Lifting,* the couple would *Drop.* Instead of *Stabilizing,* the couple would *Shake.* Instead of *Moving,* the couple would *Stop;* same couple, different principles, different outcomes. As it pertains to couples working through obstacles, double-mindedness could be described as *a disease that plagues the marriage's course of progression.* James 1:8 articulates this idea in this manner: "A double-minded man is unstable in all his ways." How the marriage thinks as one in Christ propels them through difficulties and out the other side.

One God

The transition from *Two Hearts* to ultimately *One God* is the overall true testament of God's faithfulness to His marriage covenant to man and woman. It is the continued journey of both husband and wife expressing gratitude to God's wisdom, instructions, corrections, perfect love, and grace in good times and in times of adversity. In this place, both husband and wife undoubtedly see God as their One and True Living God. Not in the sense that the two have forgotten Who God is or that He is unrecognizable. But together, the two have seen God reveal Himself mightily as a Counselor, a Comforter, a Father, and Provider, with each passing second, minute, hour, day, week, month, and year. In other words, there is an outpouring of thankfulness, gratitude, and praise to the One Who alone is worthy.

To fully express this idea, let us look at Deuteronomy 4:35—39 (NKJV), which reads: "To you, it was shown, that you might know that the Lord Himself is God; there is none other besides Him. Out of heaven, He let you hear His voice, that He might instruct you; on earth, He showed you His great fire, and you heard His words out of the midst of the fire. And because He loved your fathers, therefore He chose their descendants after them; and He brought you out of Egypt with His Presence, with His mighty power, driving out from before you nations greater and mightier than you, to bring you in, to give you their land as an inheritance, as it is this day. Therefore, know this day, and consider it in your heart, that the Lord Himself is God in heaven above and on the earth beneath; there is no other."

This scripture highlights a significant discovery I think encapsulates this nugget of truth. First, it is crucial to observe that verse 35 seems to have hit a home run with the bases loaded with this powerful statement: "To you, it was shown, that you might know that the Lord Himself is God; there is none other besides Him." Now for context, the Book of Deuteronomy is a book that mainly focuses on rehearsing or reiterating God's Laws. It is to confirm God's standards: *His way of thinking.* Deuteronomy 4:35 (NKJV) connects with the mind (heart) of the reader and tells them they *know* God. Let that sink in for a moment. You have His way of thinking, for it has been revealed to you.

Often in marriage, this *way of thinking* appears to be surrounded by opposition greater than what is *known*. The couple seems to be contending with enemies inside their camp—meaning within themselves and the outside. But it takes the God of Deuteronomy 4:35—39 to drive out these *nations,* foreign and domestic, that appears to be so much greater and mightier than the God of the marriage—a testament to the Only Living God.

I again want to reiterate that the principles that every Godly marriage honors in return will honor them. Husbands, wives embrace your spouse's uniqueness; laugh more, cherish the time you do have with them. Marriage is good when you can see it differently: *God's way.* This advantage permits the couple to discover an awareness of the marriage's overall value and preserve its worth in God's sight at all cost. So yes, God does smile seeing His man and woman that he has joined together going from *faith to faith, from glory to glory.* God takes pleasure in seeing His man and woman adopting the principle of going from *Two Hearts, One Mind, in One God* together.

"Like-Mind Connection" Wrap-Up:

1. For couples who are engaged, *lowering the mask* of your fiancé can begin with the process of premarital counseling. Is this a step in the process where you and your fiancé have strongly considered participating? If not, what are your reservations?
2. Married couples are constantly transitioning due to the maturity and development of both spouses. How has the transitioning from *Two-Hearts to One God* impressed the marriage? At any point in the marriage, were there any areas of unwillingness to adapt?
3. In what areas could you and your spouse apply the *Agree, Lift, Stabilize, and Move* methodology to overcome challenges the two of you have identified within the marriage?

Notes

1   Justin Tash. Why Divorce Is So Common in Today's Society (The Sad Truth). (2021). Retrieved from http://www.btlfamilylaw.com/why-couples-divorce/

2   Glenn T. Stanto. Divorce Rate in the Church – As High as the World. (2011, August 15). Retrieved from http://www.focusonthefamily.com/marriage/divorce-rate-in-the-church-as-high-as-the-world/

3   Siege of Jerusalem (587 BC).wikia.org, 17 January 2020, http://www.military.wikia.org/wiki/Siege_of_Jerusalem_(587_BC)

4   Honor Whiteman. Laughter releases 'feel good hormones' to promote social bonding. (2017, June 3). Retrieved from http://www.medicalnewstoday.com

5   Michael Dimock. Defining generations: Where Millennials end and Generation Z begins. (2019, January 17). Retrieved from http://pewresearch.org/fact-tank/2019/01/17/where-millennials-end-and-generation-z-begins/

6   Dr. Richard J. Krejcir. The Names of God. (2001). Retrieved from http://www.discipleshiptools.org/apps/articles/default.asp?article=47370&columnid=4192

7   Bill Chappell. U.S. National Debt Hits Record $22 Trillion. (2019, February 13). Retrieved from http://www.npr.org/2019/02/13/694199256/u-s-national-debt-hits-22-trillion-a-new-record-thats-predicted-to-fall

8   Xenos (Greek). (2020, April 22). In Wikipedia. http://www.en.wikipedia.org/wiki/Xenos_(Greek)

9   Jessica Brodie. What Every Christian Needs to Know about Koinonia. (2019, October 18). Retrieved from http://www.crosswalk.com/faith/spiritual-life/what-every-christian-needs-to-know-about-koinonia.html

10 10. Thirteen Colonies. (2021, April 19). In Wikipedia. http://www.en.wikipedia.org/wiki/Thirteen_Colonies

11 Divorce Statistics: Over 115 Studies, Facts and Rates for 2020. (2020) Retrieved from https://www.wf-lawyers.com/divorce-statistics-and-facts/

Printed in the United States
by Baker & Taylor Publisher Services